art / shop / eat

MADRID

Robert Smyth

FUENCARRAL

605

M40

M30

River Manzanares

Avenida del

Avenida de

Cardenal Herrera Oria

Ilustración

Sinesio

Delgado

M30

TETUÁN

Plaza
Castilla

Estación de
Chamartín

VI

Calle

de

CIUDAD
UNIVERSITARIA

Murillo

Bravo

Castellana

C. de
J. Ramón
Jiménez

Vergara

Estadio
Santiago
Bernabéu

C. de J. Costa

Auditor
de Mús

Príncipe

de

Museo
la Ciud

pp. 102–103

C. de
Céa Bermúdez

C. de
José Abascal

Calle

Serrano

de

p. 132

Avda

C. de F. Si

Séneca

Parque
del Oeste

C. de la Princesa

San
Bernardo

Calle Santa Engracia

de

C. de Génova

de

SALAMANCA

Calle

Calle o

Casa de Campo

Teleférico de Madrid

S. Antonio
de la Florida

Templo
de Debod

Centro Cultural
Conde Duque

Plaza de
España

CENTRO

Gran

Vía

Plaza de
Cibeles

Calle

de

Estación
Príncipe Pío

Palacio Real

Catedral
de la Almudena

Puerta
del Sol

Plaza
Mayor

Thyssen-
Bornemisza

P. del Prado

Prado

Parque
del Retiro

Parque
de Atracciones

de

Portugal

Carpetana

Avenida

ARGANZUELA

Reina Sofía

Estación
de Atocha

pp. 8–

V

Vía

LATINA

p. 68

P. De Santa María de la Cabeza

M30

Estación Sur
de Autobuses

River Manzanares

Avda. de Córdoba

Avd

CARABANCHEL

401

2

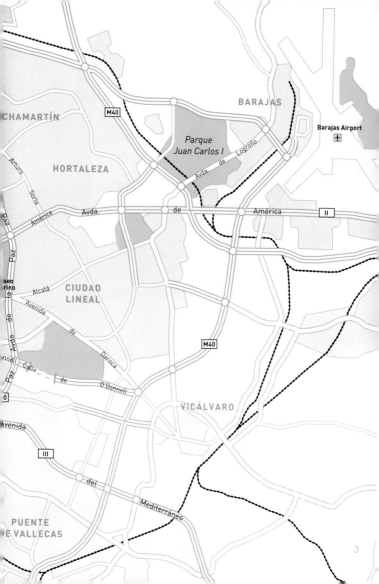

CHAMARTÍN

BARAJAS

M40

Parque
Juan Carlos I

Barajas Airport

HORTALEZA

Avda. de Logroño

Avda. de América

II

Arturo

Soria

América

Paz

Paz

seo
rino

Atcalá

CIUDAD
LINEAL

Avenida

de

Daroca

M40

Avda.

nnell

Calle de O'Donnell

Paz

0

VICÁLVARO

venida

III

del

Mediterráneo

PUENTE
E VALLECAS

3

Paseo del Arte

Old Madrid

Chueca & Malasaña

Salamanca & Recoletos

Trips out of Town

CONTENTS

introduction

Madrid lays an ever more convincing claim to being the art capital of Europe. Three top art museums—the Prado, Thyssen Bornemisza and the Reina Sofía—lie within a few hundred metres of each other. And alongside their truly astounding collections, there are secretive gems tucked away in more obscure corners, like peaceful monasteries one step away from the heart of the action.

Madrid is a shop 'til you drop kind of town, with swathes of cutting edge designer shops, colourful markets and old-fashioned *tiendas* set back in time.

Perhaps because the city lies at the geographical heart of Spain, it is also the epicentre of Spanish culture and cuisine, drawing from all corners of the country's diverse regions, and turning itself into a unique and sublime cocktail of experiences. If Spain is sometimes dubbed 'las Españas'—the Spains—rather than one single Spain, you could just as well talk about its capital in the plural too: there is something here for everyone.

Though it may lack the ancient architecture so ubiquitous in other parts of Spain, or the giddy *Modernismo* of Barcelona, eclectic Madrid has an allure all of its own. For a touch of the really ancient, though, take a train to nearby Toledo, the heart of medieval Spain, and sometime capital of the realm.

In fact there is a terrific range of destinations within easy striking distance of the city. There's really no excuse for not getting in on the action.

PASEO DEL ARTE

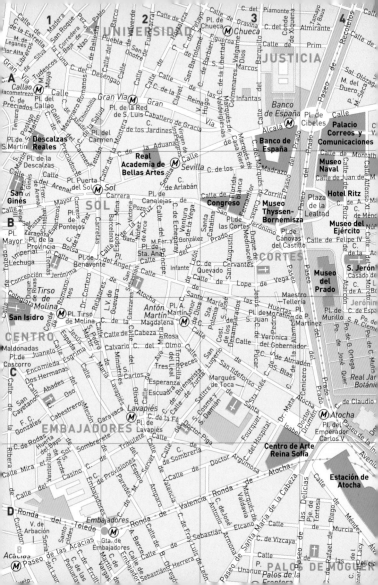

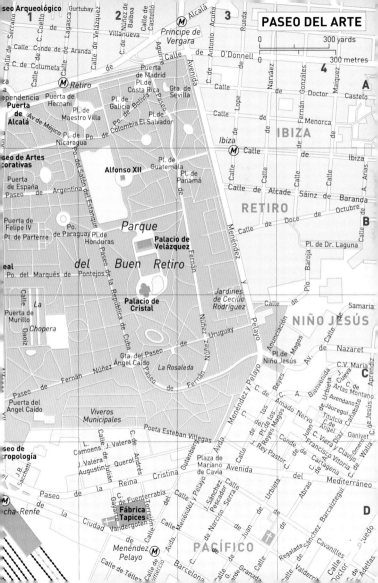

PASEO DEL ARTE

Many visitors simply never stray beyond the artistically stacked Paseo del Arte, with the world class Prado, Reina Sofía and the Thyssen-Bornemisza art museums. While this might not be doing Madrid the full justice it deserves, it must be said this area has an incredible amount to offer. Without having to move far and with minimum hassle you can take in some of the very best paintings in the entire history of recorded art, relax in botanic gardens or the grand expanse of the Retiro—or even in the gardens of Atocha station—and then adjourn for something to eat or drink, for which there's a staggering choice.

Once away from the art, a good time or a great feed is never far away, as the streets spreading off Santa Ana and around Huertas are packed with restaurants and bars. An altogether more local experience is also on hand. Just a few streets on from the increasingly stag party-infested Santa Ana and Huertas zone, Lavapiés is much more authentic. This predominantly working-class area is a mostly harmonious multi-cultural melting pot of immigrants and locals, with some classic drinking dens and tapas bars for those prepared to seek them out.

THE BIG THREE

Three monumental art museums, situated within minutes of each other, make Madrid the ideal art destination. The art owned by Madrid's top three museums is truly mesmerising, and the galleries themselves are expanding, upping the exhibition space considerably (due for completion in 2006). An anomaly of the Prado had long been the fact that ten times as many paintings were in storage than on show. As we speak, the floorspace of the three museums is being expanded by a gigantic 50,000 square metres.

The combined collections of the three museums take the visitor from the Renaissance and El Greco to Picasso and Pop Art.

TICKETS

For those wanting to visit all three art museums, which is probably just about everybody, it's well worth picking up an *Abono Paseo del Arte* ticket (€7.66) with which you can visit each of the three once within the year of purchase.

For those who get addicted, at least for the meantime, there's the *Tarjeta anual múltiple* that costs €36.06, which gives unlimited access to all three for the duration of a year.

Museo del Prado

OPEN	Tues–Sun 9am–7pm, 24 & 31 Dec 9am–2pm
CLOSED	Mondays; 1/1, Good Friday, 1/5, 25/12
CHARGES	Permanent collection: €6; €3 reduced admission, Free Sun 9 am–7pm, 2/6, 18/6, 12/10, 6/12 (NB: the Prado can get very crowded on these days). Temporary exhibitions sometimes included in general admission ticket. Free admission ticket for over 65s and under 18s.
TELEPHONE	91 330 28 00
WEB	www.museoprado.mcu.es
MAIN ENTRANCE	Edificio Villanueva, Paseo del Prado
DISABLED ACCESS	Yes
METRO	Banco de España and Atocha
SERVICES	Large shop, café and restaurant

HIGHLIGHTS

Peter Paul Rubens: *Adoration of the Magi*

Diego Velázquez: *Las Meninas*

Hieronymus Bosch: *The Garden of Delights*

Goya: *Tres de Mayo 1808: the Executions on Príncipe Pío Hill*

The Prado is one of the world's finest art museums, and it pays to approach the numerous gems of its collection with respect and discernment, instead of like a child let loose in a sweet shop. This is certainly one place where it makes no sense to try and see everything on a single visit, or you risk biting off more fine art than you can chew.

NB: Many of the best pictures do move around at the Prado and in the recent temporary exhibition extraordinaire, 'The Spanish Portrait: From El Greco to Picasso', 50% of the paintings were shifted from their usual positions.

THE PERMANENT COLLECTION

There's simply no obvious route around the Prado. One mode of attack is to pick out which school of art to expend your energies on. The collection gathered by the Spanish crown over the centuries is quite eclectic and is by no means a comprehensive history of art. Nevertheless it excels in what it has. It boasts the largest and greatest collection in the world of Spanish art up to the late 19th century. The Flemish and Italian schools are also very well represented, with works acquired from these outposts of the once mighty Spanish Empire.

What follows is a summary of some of the works that are simply not to be missed.

SPANISH SCHOOL FROM 1100 TO 1850

Entering the Ground Floor from the Puerta de Goya you'll pass 12th-century Spanish murals [51c] plucked from the Santa Cruz chapel in Maderuelo, Segovia and the 11th-century Mozarabic church from the province of Soria.

El Greco 'The Greek' (born Domenicos Theotocopoulos on Crete) and taken by the Spanish as one of their very own, has three rooms devoted to him [60A, 61A, 62A]. He lived in Toledo from 1577 to his death in 1614, turning out epic, brooding works that quite simply moved Spanish, if not European portrait painting up a few gears. In El Greco's portraits look out for his focus on the face and hands of the subjects and the general omission of other detail, especially in the instantly recognisable *Nobleman with his Hand on his Chest*.

His work can also appear to come from another world. In the fervently spiritual *Adoration of the Shepherds*, which was painted for the chapel in which he was laid to rest, the light radiating from the baby Christ appears to bring vivid colour to the other characters.

Royal portraits by **Alonso Sánchez Coello** hang in the next room [63A].

The best works of **Diego Velázquez**, for many Spain's greatest painter if not the greatest painter of them all, can be found on the first floor [12, 14, 15, 15A]. *Las Meninas* ('The Ladies in Waiting'), is certainly the most celebrated amongst the Prado's scores of masterpieces. It was painted in Velázquez's studio in the Alcázar and is an intricate work of contrasting figures. In the foreground Infanta Margarita is attended by her ladies-in-waiting Agustina Sarmiento, Isabel de Solís and the dwarves Mari Bárbola and Nicolasito Perusato. Their guardian Marcela de Ulloa and this time a gentleman-in-waiting stand behind watching over them. To the side Velázquez can be seen in front of an enormous canvas, seemingly regarding the youngsters. He is wearing the red cross of Santiago, which must have been added later as he was not made a knight of the order of Santiago until 1658. *Las Meninas* was painted in 1656.

To make matters more interesting José Nito, the queen's chamberlain, stands watching the scene on the stairs outside the door. To cap it all, King Felipe IV and his wife Mariana of Austria, who are supposedly the ones posing for the court painter, are reflected in the mirror centre rear. The flawless Velázquez himself

Velázquez: *Las Meninas* (1656)

is perhaps guilty of a touch of vanity, shaving quite a few years off his own appearance—the young dandy portrayed was actually 57 years old at the time.

Velázquez's dramatic account of the historic Spanish military defeat of the Dutch *The Surrender of Breda* or *The Lances* shows the victorious Ambrosio Spanola taking the key to the town of

Breda from Justin of Nassau. The winners and the losers are portrayed in incredible detail. It was painted for the Hall of Realms in the Buen Retiro Palace.

The military theme is continued with the *Count-Duke of Olivares on Horseback*, which is thought to come from the 1638 Battle of Fuenterrabía, though ironically the porky count himself did not take up arms. Nevertheless, it was important to him to demonstrate that he had been there. The Spanish aristocracy behaved in cases like this like many a Stalinist politician after them, who would have themselves airbrushed into and out of photographs to prove their politically important presence at or absence from rallies and events.

The mythological and humorous aspect of *The Triumph of Bacchus* or *Los Borrachos* ('The Drunkards') is purported to have been influenced by the Flemish painter Rubens during a trip to Madrid in 1628–29.

Works by renowned Seville artist **Murillo**, a realist painter of mystical religious figures, such as *The Good Shepherd*—portrayed as a child—are also on the first floor [29]. His *Immaculate Conception of Soult* (named after the Maréchal de Soult, the Napoleonic commander who removed it to the Louvre during the Spanish War of Independence) portrays the Virgin as a beautiful young woman dressed in white and blue, surrounded by clouds and angels, standing on a serpent (symbol of the devil) and a crescent moon, a reference to the Book of Revelation: 'and there appeared a great wonder in heaven; a woman clothed with the sun, and the moon under her feet; and the dragon stood before the woman. And she brought forth a man child, who was to rule all nations with a rod of iron. And the dragon was cast out'.

Murillo actually died painting in 1682, crushed beneath scaffolding while working in a convent in Cadiz. His contemporaries—Alonso Cano, Carreño, Claudio Coello and Valdés Leal—are also exhibited.

Look out for the superbly detailed still lifes of 18th-century Spanish painter **Luis Meléndez** in the adjacent wing [19].

The Prado extension: she just gets bigger

The Prado, originally built as a science museum, is currently undergoing its most ambitious expansion scheme to date. Pritzker Prize-winning Spanish architect Rafael Moneo is connecting the Villanueva building with a new building and the rebuilt cloister of Los Jerónimos monastery, a project which has raised its fair share of controversy. The new Prado will link the previous 19th-century building with a partly underground cement-and-glass contemporary complex containing the monastery, whose reconstruction under a glass roof has prompted protests from local residents. Moneo is concealing the link between the old and new buildings under a roof garden that is to recall the landscaped garden that earlier existed in the same spot.

The new space will comprise space for temporary exhibitions, a lecture theatre, conservation studios, a café, restaurant and offices. Thus the original building will be significantly freed up and will allow the main hall with its apse to be seen as Villanueva originally intended.

El Casón del Buen Retiro, which overlooks Madrid's expansive Retiro park, and which has been home to the Prado's 19th-century painting and sculpture, is currently closed for reorganization. The 19th-century work is due to be incorporated into the permanent collection.

The Prado will celebrate its rebirth by promoting its remarkable permanent collection as well as presenting its new exhibition space dubbed the Garden of Earthly Delights. The new galleries in the Jerónimos building will display works as part of its Modern Masters exhibition.

GOYA AT THE PRADO

The Prado's collection of Goya is quite exceptional, amounting to some 135 paintings, 50 cartoons used for tapestries, and many sketches. Today he is perhaps most famous as a chronicler of historical events. His depiction of French reprisals on the Madrid uprising in *Tres de Mayo 1808: the Executions on Príncipe Pío Hill*

MUSEO DEL PRADO
GROUND FLOOR

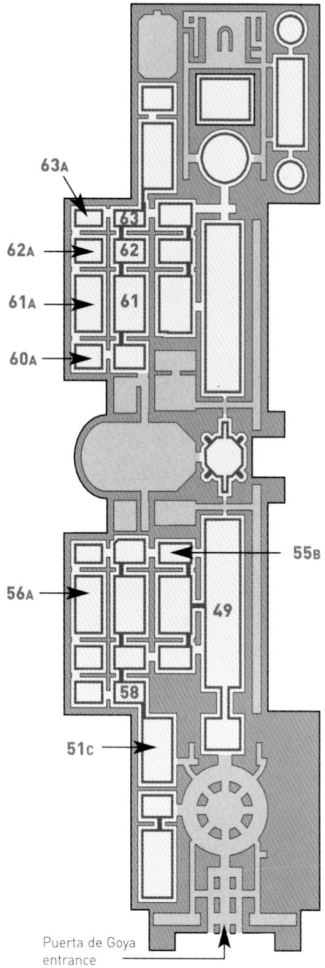

63A

62A

61A

60A

63

62

61

60

55B

56A

49

58

51C

HIGHLIGHTS

El Greco: 60A, 61A, 62A
Bosch: 56A
Titian: 61, 62, 63
Dürer: 55B

Puerta de Goya
entrance

MUSEO DEL PRADO
FIRST FLOOR

39

19

29

15A → **15**

14

12

10A → **10**

9

9B

8A → **8**

7

3

HIGHLIGHTS

Velázquez: 12, 14, 15, 15A
Murillo: 29
Goya: 39
Rubens: 8, 9, 9B, 10

[39] is a startling anti-war statement that has lost none of its impact despite the passage of nearly two hundred years. The indignity and helplessness portrayed on the face of the protagonist, who is highlighted out of the encompassing darkness as the firing squad press on with the slaughter unperturbed, is a moment captured in time. It was, however, painted six years after the event, in tandem with the overthrow of the French occupiers, to usher in the return to Madrid of King Fernando VII. Whether Goya sought to win back the favour of the returning Spanish royal house through the painting is a question actually rendered unimportant given the artistic significance of this work. Some art critics say that Expressionism started here.

Goya in fact got his start in Madrid as a tapestry cartoon painter at the Santa Barbara Royal Tapestry Factory, which produced tapestries for the copious royal holdings. *The Wine Harvest*, representing autumn as part of a quartet of pictures portraying the seasons of the year in Room 94 on the second floor, was painted by Goya for Carlos III's dining room at the El Pardo Palace. The other paintings representing the other seasons can be found in the hall. Note how the colours are clearly divided to enable the weavers to get on with their job of creating the tapestry from Goya's marvellous cartoon. It even contains a painting within a painting. The Prado itself points out that the basket on the head of one of the figures is considered one of the finest Spanish still lifes.

Goya's supreme versatility is expressed magnificently in the contrasting portraits of the *Nude Maja* and the *Clothed Maja* in Room 89, also on the second floor. The clothed version, with its fluid and sensual brushwork, is just as revealing as the stark naked portrayal.

Goya is also noted for portraying the Spanish royal family as he saw them and not as he was supposed to see them, and with his deft and subtle touch he easily got away with it.

In *Carlos IV and his Family* painted in 1800, the king is an almost peripheral and unfocused overweight figure while his queen—Maria Luisa—takes centre stage and with it control of the royal family, which is believed to reflect the real situation perfectly.

Goya: *Tres de Mayo 1808: The Executions on Príncipe Pío Hill* (1814)

There's also a tribute on the part of Goya to Velázquez, one of Goya's biggest influences, with the inclusion of Goya himself in the painting, echoing what Velázquez himself did in *Las Meninas*. The use of light in the painting anticipates the Impressionist movement nearly a century later.

Nevertheless, though there is no record that the king or queen were displeased with the work, this proved to be Goya's last royal portrait.

Goya's notorious and chilling, though still artistically brilliant, black paintings were etched straight into the walls of his house by the River Manzanares, where he lived out his last decade, isolated by deafness. The works were not transferred to canvas until long after his death. They are exhibited on a rotating basis in the Goya Drawings Gallery on the second floor. The alarming *Saturn Devouring one of his Sons* occupied the wall of Goya's dining room and represents the god consuming his biggest threat, symbolising life ultimately destroying all that it creates.

THE FLEMISH SCHOOL FROM 1430 TO 1700

The Prado houses some of **Hieronymus Bosch**'s (known as 'El Bosco' in Spanish) most futuristic creations [56A]. His *Garden of Delights* is possibly the Prado's most viewed exhibit. Visitors gaze at this wondrous—though somewhat elusive—panelled painting trying to make sense of it. The enigmatic nature of the work as well as its remarkable diversion from the artistic norm of the age is what makes it so deeply fascinating. The left panel apparently depicts the creation of mankind, while in the middle and largest section the human race indulges in earthly pleasures. In the right panel they get their just deserts for their carnal exploits: eternal hell fire. In Bosch's vision of hell humans are dissected, consumed whole by bizarre birdlike creatures—and that's just for starters. Bosch's dark, destructive background tones, broken by visions of carnage, even evoke images of the Blitzkrieg some half a millennium later. Continuing the theme of Bosch's unique and seeming insight into the future, on the right panel in his *Adoration of the Magi*, in the middle of the lake, the town looks very much like a modern cityscape and hardly like a 16th-century Flemish town.

Bosch's *Table of the Seven Deadly Sins* is unfortunately no longer exhibited horizontally as a table but on the wall like any other painting, meaning that parts of it are upside down. The irregular-formatted work has a circular layout with God in the centre, by whose all-seeing eye no single sin goes unnoticed. Scenes of the deathbed, the Last Judgment, heaven, and hell surround Him.

Joachim Pateniers's *Charon crossing the Styx* is more restrained that Bosch's vision, though it oozes a sinister mystery all its own.

Pieter Brueghel the Elder's graphically detailed *Triumph of Death* hangs on the opposite wall to *The Garden of Delights* [56A]. Amidst a scorched and parched landscape an unrelenting army of unceasing hordes of skeletons cuts down helpless humans in cold blood as death wins through in the end, reminding us that we are all ultimately doomed. One skeleton holds an hour glass in front of a king to let him know that his time is nigh, as well as conveying a more comforting message for most of us: i.e. that rank and position count for little in the final reckoning.

Works by 15th-century artist **Rogier van der Weyden** are displayed nearby [58], including the striking and brightly coloured cross shaped *Deposition*, in which Jesus is taken down from the cross surrounded by weeping mourners.

For a unique collaboration it's hard to beat *The Five Senses*, a veritable tour de force of different artistic genres from Jan 'Velvet' Brueghel (1568–1625), the son of Pieter Brueghel the Elder and another Prado favourite Peter Paul Rubens (1577–1640). **Jan Brueghel** earned the nickname 'Velvet' from his skill in rendering texture. Rubens was a close friend, and the two often collaborated. In this case it was Rubens who painted the allegorical figures. The Prado has some 100 other works by **Rubens**, chiefly on the first floor, where there are three rooms [8, 9, 10] concentrating on his oeuvre.

Rubens's classic *Adoration of the Magi* actually played a role in the brokering of peace between Spain and the Low Countries. It was commissioned in 1609 to be hung in the room in Antwerp Town Hall where successful peace negotiations took place leading to more than a dozen years of amnesty between the warring powers. The painting later ended up in Spain and Rubens, unhappy with what he saw on a visit here toward the end of the 1620s, decided to breathe new life into it. The artistically opulent result is too detailed to describe in short, though it's easy to see why it is considered one of his masterworks. The rider on the right is Rubens himself.

The *Combat between Saint George and the Dragon* [9в] is an example of one of the works from Rubens's youth, radiating with promise and the skilful use of glorious bright colours. His *Three Graces* [9] features portraits of his two wives.

The wonderfully mystic *Andromeda Freed by Perseus*, in which Perseus appears as a 17th-century Spanish knight, was his final and unfinished work, with **Jacob Jordaens** ably applying the final touches. Look out for Antwerp artist Jordaens' own works as well [8A], which include a *Family Portrait* from c.1623.

Excellent **Van Dyck** portraits include *Martin Ryckaert*, *The Musician Liberti*, and *Count Henry de Bergh* [10A]. There's also one of himself portrayed next to his protector Sir Endymion Porter.

THE ITALIAN SCHOOL FROM 1300 TO 1800

Instantly attention-grabbing are **Botticelli**'s three panels of *The Story of Nastagio degli Onesti* (1483), illustration of the eighth story of the fifth day, 'Hell for Cruel Lovers', from Boccaccio's *Decameron* [49]. A naked woman is relentlessly pursued by a rider and a pack of hounds, who tear out her heart and eat it. She then stands to her feet and runs away, and the grisly chase begins again. The story goes that the woman spurned the young man's love, and thus is doomed to be chased by him forever, as he tries to seize her heart. The fourth panel—in which the woman at last gives in to her pursuer—is in private hands in the US.

Room 49 is also notable for the impressive collection of **Raphael** (1483–1520). These include his early Leonardo-influenced Florentine work *The Holy Family with a Lamb* (1507), the superbly captured but unidentified *Portrait of a Cardinal* from around 1510, and *Christ Falls on the Way to Calvary*. The latter was painted in Rome in 1517, for the Benedictine convent of Santa Maria dello Spasimo in Palermo, Sicily, from where it gets its more common name *El Pasmo de Sicilia* ('The Wonder of Sicily').

The great **Titian**, who resided in Spain serving stints for Emperor Charles V and King Philip II, is exhibited on the ground floor [61, 62, 63]. *The Emperor Charles V in Mühlberg* was captured on canvas following the 1547 battle when Charles V emerged victorious over the Protestants. Titian's religious works include *Ecce Homo* and *The Glory*, while mythological works include *Bacchanal*, *Venus and Adonis* and the *Garden of Loves* or *Worship of Venus*. The subject of this last is thought to come from the 3rd-century Greek writer Philostratus. The painting depicts countless baby cupids feeding each other apples and playing while watched over by Venus herself and two serving women. *Danae Receiving the Golden Rain* depicts Zeus transforming himself into golden rain to seduce the delectable Danae, whose father had put her under lock and key. The *Self-portrait* was painted when Titian was around 80.

Tiepolo can be found on the second floor; he served for a time as painter to the Spanish court.

THE BEST OF THE REST

Many works are displayed from the German School from 1450 to 1800. The collection is especially notable for the paintings of **Albrecht Dürer [55B]**. His two portraits of Adam and Eve, painted in 1507, made it into the Royal Collection courtesy of Queen Christina of Sweden, who gave them to Felipe IV.

Anton Raphael Mengs (1728–79), court painter to Carlos III, is exhibited in Room 82 on the second floor. His works are skilful though not particularly original or pioneering.

The French School includes work from 17th-century painter **Nicholas Poussin**, who was strongly influenced by Italian Renaissance painters Raphael and Titian [3]. Poussin's *Parnassus* is a landscape painting that uses his characteristically intense colours and classical composition style to the full, so much so that the trees in the background are almost like Roman columns.

For the Dutch School, Rembrandt's 1634 masterpiece *Artemisia* [7] is the only work that the Prado claims as an acknowledged **Rembrandt**. The self-portrait is now regarded to be a copy.

Of the British School, there are two paintings by **Joshua Reynolds**: *Portrait of a Clergyman* and *Portrait of Mr James Bourdieu*, and **Thomas Gainsborough**'s *Dr Isaac Henrique Seqeira* and *Mr Robert Butcher of Walthamstan* in Room 83 on the second floor.

The Dauphin's Treasure (Tesoro del Delfín), some very rich pickings which once belonged to Louis le Grand Dauphin, son of Louis XIV and father of Spain's very first Bourbon king Felipe V, is exhibited in the basement.

Museo Nacional Centro de Arte Reina Sofía

OPEN	Mon–Sat 10am–9pm, Sun 10am–2.30pm
CLOSED	Tuesdays
CHARGES	€3.01; €1.5 reduced admission, free on Saturdays 2.30pm–9pm, Sundays 10am–2.30pm and 18/6, 12/10, 6/12 Temporary exhibitions included in admission. Free admission for over 65s and under 18s
TELEPHONE	91 468 30 02
WEB	www.museoreinasofia.mcu.es
MAIN ENTRANCE	C/Santa Isabel 52
DISABLED ACCESS	Yes
METRO	Atocha
SERVICES	Small gift shop by entrance, large shop in basement. Café and restaurant

HIGHLIGHTS

Picasso's *Guernica*

Retrato de Josette **by Juan Gris**

Joan Miró's *Man with a Pipe*

Salvador Dalí's *El gran masturbador*

Francis Bacon's *Tumbling Figure*

The Reina Sofía opened as an art museum in 1992. The building originally came into being from Felipe V's desire to create a hospital in Madrid under the auspices of the crown. Work began in March 1758 and ten years into the project architect died, which saw Madrid's favourite architect Francesco Sabatini come on board.

The former hospital provides a fantastic setting for the display of some exceptional works of art. Its sometimes quite lonely passageways and spacious rooms give the visitor the space to contemplate the works that brilliantly and clearly reveal the tendencies of Spanish and international art over the last hundred or more years. Super-cool elevators propel you upwards to a rare art experience as you look onto the plaza below, where children kick a football around.

SECOND FLOOR

The collection begins here, with the development of Spanish art and its global relevance from the late 19th century to after the Second World War. Room 1 traces the origins of modernity in Spanish contemporary art, led by a handful of Basque painters, and by the great Catalans Ramón Casas, Santiago Rusiñol and Isidre Nonell. While Casas and Rusiñol drew clear inspiration from contemporary French art and the bohemian ideal, the short-lived, tempestuous, expressionistic Nonell drew on life's outcasts, painting highly charged images of gypsies and of the mentally handicapped. José Gutiérrez Solana, a painter from Madrid, has a room all to himself [2]. His *Gathering at the Café Pombo* (1920) portrays the classic Madrid pastime of the *tertulia*—intellectuals engaging in lively debate—which thrived in the city around the turn of the last century. Solana is one of the group, and the picture was donated by the writer Gómez de la Serna, who was the leader of the circle. The next room [3] explores the various avant-garde movements—Vibracionismo, Constructivism, Simultaneismo and Cubism—that sprang up in Spain around the beginning of the 20th century.

The following room [4] is home to another Madrid artist, Juan Gris, a key mover and somewhat underrated participant in the Cubist movement, and who—unfortunately for 20th-century art—died at just 40 in 1927. The *Retrato de Josette* painted in 1916, and *Guitar in front of the Sea* (1925), are both seminal works. Gris and Picasso both lived in Paris and were key figures in Cubism; it was Gris who brilliantly captured Picasso on canvas in perfect Cubist tones. His *Homage to Picasso* normally hangs in Chicago, but comes to Madrid sometimes for temporary exhibitions.

MUSEO NACIONAL CENTRO DE ARTE REINA SOFÍA
SECOND FLOOR

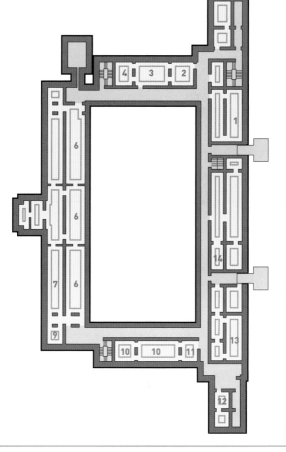

Pablo Picasso: *Woman in Blue* (1901)

Many visitors to the Reina Sofía head straight for Picasso's epic anti-war masterpiece, *Guernica* [6].

Guernica

Guernica was painted for the Spanish Pavilion at the 1937 Paris World Fair. Sketches of the distraught and tortured figures incorporated into the painting complement the finished work. Picasso received criticism from some quarters for the picture being a bit too enigmatic to represent the plight of the Basque people, the victims of German Nazi bombings conducted almost as a favour: Franco, the Spanish dictator, made an appalling barter with the Nazis, allowing the Luftwaffe to road-test their bombs on the Basque village. Allied to this is the question of the larger plight of free Spain. Few, however, can dispute the work's striking originality. The figures actually come from bullfighting, a dominant theme for Picasso around this time.

Picasso hoped the painting would find its rightful home in the Prado; more recently the Guggenheim in Bilbao staked a claim, highlighting the painting's Basque association.

Besides this great masterpiece the Reina Sofía possesses other outstanding **Picasso** creations.

Woman in Blue (*pictured opposite*) was painted on a short stay in Madrid in 1901 when Picasso was just 20. Painted in a more conventional Realist style, it demonstrates Picasso's skill as a draughtsman, and how technically gifted he was at handling paint. The *Still Life* (*The Dead Birds*), painted over a decade later, comes from his Synthetic Cubism period, and was one of the first artistic works to use fragments of paper.

Starring in in the adjacent room [7] is the almost-as-famous Catalan artist **Joan Miró**. His early *Man with a Pipe*, painted in 1925, with its alien-like figure, could even be said to be one of the more conventional works from this pioneering artist. Miró's later works include the 1970 *Woman, Bird and Star* (*Homage to Picasso*). His paintings are broken up by the sculptures of fellow Catalan Julio González. Miró's own sculpture is also on show [16].

La mujer en el jardín (1929–30), González's collaboration with Picasso, is an important sculpture, while sculptures by David Smith, and the photographs taken by Dora Maar chronicling the creation of *Guernica*, are also worth a look.

Moving into the corner room **[9]**, works by Alexander Calder, Jean Arp and Vassily Kandinsky, and the Spanish artist, writer and musician Eugenio Granell are juxtaposed to illustrate the huge variety of stylistic expression covered by the terms Surrealism and Abstraction.

The next suite of rooms **[10–11]** contain key works by the weird and wonderful **Salvador Dalí** from the early 20s and through the 30s when his Surrealism excelled. Landmark works like *Cenicitas* (1928) and the daringly titled *El gran masturbador* (1929) are purposely followed by Dalí's international contemporaries including Max Ernst, Yves Tanguy and René Magritte, intended to show Dalí against a backdrop of what was being produced in the world around him.

Rather appropriately Dalí is followed **[12]** by some of his partners in crime. Aragonese film director Luis Buñuel's *Un Chien Andalu*, the concept for which Dalí helped him with, can be seen in the film theatre. There's also work by the poet Rafael Alberti and playwright Federico García Lorca.

Beyond this a separate room **[13]** chronicles avante-garde movements in Spanish art in the 1920s and 1930s. There are some good examples of sculpture by the great Aragonese exponent of Novecentismo Pablo Gargallo, who was a close friend of both Picasso and Gris. There are also examples of Spanish interwar realism, and neo-Cubist work by a number of artists, most important of whom is perhaps Benjamín Palencia. Palencia was the founder of the so-called Vallecas School, and was instrumental in reuniting Spanish art with the Hispanic tradition, taking the Castilian landscape as his inspiration.

Luis Fernández (1900–73), an Asturian painter who resided in Paris and liaised with the likes of Picasso and Braque, is exhibited in the next section **[14]** and is followed by more works by Benjamín Palencia pitched against the sculpture of Alberto

Sánchez, co-founder of the Vallecas School. Sánchez's sculptures are chiefly geometrical, and have been described as having one eye on the future and the other on the classical past.

FOURTH FLOOR

The fourth floor concentrates on artistic developments and schools from the late 40s to the present. Post Civil War Spanish art saw a new approach to the concept of landscape painting, as can be seen in the work of Juan Manuel Díaz Caneja [18], with his ground-breaking takes on the Madrid cityscape.

Next door [19], works from two cutting edge 20th-century schools: the Abstract Expressionist Pórtico, and Dau al Set, a Catalan group that revived Surrealism, are exhibited. Antoni Tàpies, Spain's greatest living contemporary artist, and now the elder statesmen of the Spanish art world, was a prime mover in Dau al Set. His *Character* is exhibited here.

The rooms in the adjacent wing [20–23] chart the rise of abstract art in Spain with works from the 1950s to the early 60s including Geometrical Abstraction by the great Basque sculptor Jorge Oteiza. There are also paintings by the five artists making up Equipo 57, whose primary concern was in exploring the role of the artist in society.

Three rooms around the corner [24–26] focus on the development of Spanish avante-garde art during the 60s and early 70s, comparing and contrasting it with what was going on elsewhere in European at the same time. Room 24 is highly notable for Francis Bacon's *Tumbling Figure*, one of those painting that considerably changes form and even meaning from close up and further away, as well as for works by fellow British artists Henry Moore and Graham Sutherland. Creations by Pierre Alechinsky and Asger Jorn, leading members of COBRA, a key mover in Abstract Expressionism, are also on show.

Leading lights of the European Group Zero, Yves Klein (Room 25) and Lucio Fontana, who both worked with monochrome, are exhibited in Room 25 and Room 26 respectively.

MUSEO NACIONAL CENTRO DE ARTE REINA SOFÍA
FOURTH FLOOR

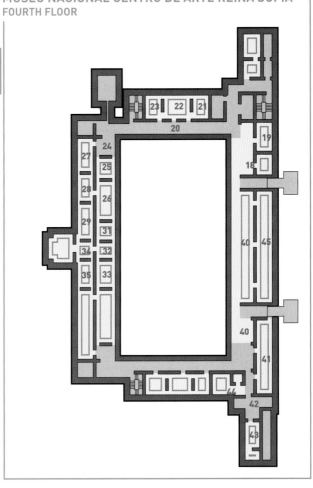

Another room [27] features work by Rafael Canogar, Martín Chirino, Luis Feito and Manuel Viola of the El Paso group, which was founded in Madrid in 1957. The Cuenca group, also represented here, was founded in the city of the same name in 1966, by Manila-born Fernando Zóbel, one of the greatest Spanish abstract artists of the 20th century, whose blurred masterpieces make you feel like you need your eyes tested.

Beyond this [28–29] is a selection of work by Manolo Millares, Manuel Rivera and the powerful and chaotic art of Antonio Saura, while the impressive Realist painter Antonio López—hyper-realist in fact, his works painted with an often photographic precision—is exhibited separately [31].

The following suite of rooms [32–35] are devoted to art after the Second World War. Notable are works by Pablo Palazuelo, an artist who originally trained as an architect, hence his preoccupation with geometry and its artistic application. Antoni Tàpies, acknowledged as the greatest living Spanish artist, has a room to himself [34], displaying some of his hallmark 'material pictures', paintings where colour and texture are subordinate to the form of the material (sand, clay, straw, rags, *objets trouvés*). Tàpies' use of such poor materials had a considerable influence on the Arte Povera movement, which also has wallspace here. Arte Povera's credo was that great art could be created from seemingly worthless media.

The wing opposite [40–45] is devoted to works from the 80s to the millennium and beyond, in a variety of genres: painting, sculpture, installation, photography and video. Look out for the great contemporary artist Eduardo Chillida [42–43]. Like Palazuelo (who was a close friend), Chillida also began life as an architect. He is best known for his monumental, geometric sculptures.

THE EXTENSION

'In the shadow of Sabatini', the famed French architect Jean Nouvel's Reina Sofía extension, consists of the construction of three adjacent buildings, extending the original display area by

50%. Nouvel uses a blade-like roof to cover the adjoining triangular site, with a central atrium open to the street, involving no disruption to the former hospital. His work turns a formerly predominantly 18th-century building into a pyramid of steel and glass, with a stain of red light showing on its transparent façade.

Tucked away in the basement, the Reina Sofía restaurant typically serves 5 *menús del día* for approx. €12 each, plus *bocadillos*, *pinchos* and canapés for those who just want a light snack. The large courtyard garden has a couple of sculptures for you to contemplate as you munch.

Museo Thyssen-Bornemisza

OPEN	Tues–Sun 10am–7pm
CLOSED	Mon; 1/1, 1/5, 25/12
CHARGES	Permanent collection: €6; €4 reduced admission. Temporary exhibitions: max €6; €4 reduced admission. Combined Ticket: €10; €6 reduced admission. Reduced admission ticket for senior citizens and students. Multiple entry for the course of the day when the entry ticket is valid. Free for children under 12 accompanied by an adult
TELEPHONE	91 369 01 51.
WEB	www.museothyssen.org
MAIN ENTRANCE	Paseo del Prado 8
DISABLED ACCESS	There is good access for visitors with disabilities and wheelchairs are available
METRO	Banco de España
SERVICES	Large shops with a wide range exclusive design, inspired by the paintings present in the Collection. Silk products, T-shirts, stationery, jewellery, ceramics. Café and restaurant serving pastries, sandwiches, mixed dishes, and à la carte.

HIGHLIGHTS

Hans Holbein the Younger – *Portrait of King Henry VIII*

José de Ribera – *Lamentation*

Edouard Manet – *Woman in a Riding Habit*

Roy Lichtenstein – *Woman in a Bath*

The Thyssen-Bornemisza is a wonderfully comprehensive collection covering the major epochs of European art over 700 years, as well as a terrific representation of 20th-century movements. It also serves perfectly to cement what's been taken in at the Prado and Reina Sofía and moves smoothly from one era to the next keeping the art lover's interest all the way. Having basked happily in the shadow of the Prado for a number of years, the Thyssen has recently turned itself into even more of a presence, adding the collection of Baron Thyssen's wife Carmen Cervera.

A FINE ART ROMANCE

The museum was first inaugurated in 1992, after the late Baron Hans Heinrich Thyssen-Bornemisza's Spanish wife Carmen Cervera persuaded him to sell his family collection to the Spanish state for a nominal price. Earlier, when Hans Heinrich inherited the family collection, he added to those areas of art that had been of less interest to his father: namely the art movements of the 19th and 20th centuries. While he still acquired works from old masters, he focused on Impressionism, Post-Impressionism, Fauvism, the German Expressionist movements, the European avant-gardes and European and American post-war art.

Monet, Van Gogh, Picasso, Mondrian, Bacon and Lichtenstein are among the key figures who feature here.

Since 2004, the museum has exhibited more than 200 additional paintings from the private collection of Carmen Cervera, a former Miss Spain who became an art expert. Before the addition of Cervera's collection, which is on loan to Spain free of charge until

2013, the Thyssen offered the most comprehensive tour through major art movements and made up for some of the areas lacking in the other two. Now it's even better.

The Carmen Thyssen-Bornemisza Collection was added alongside the permanent collection and opened for show in mid-2004. Architects Manuel Baquero and Robert Brufau and the Estudio BOPBAA—Josep Bohigas Arnau, Francesc Pla Ferrer and Iñaki Baquero—fused two adjoining buildings harmoniously into the Palacio de Villahermosa which has housed the original Thyssen-Bornemisza collection since 1993. Today, from the inside you would hardly know that they were ever separated. Arranged as a logical continuation of the Palacio de Villahermosa, the fixed part of the collection may eventually be merged into original collection, but for now Carmen's and her Baron's lie side by side. Sadly, he did not live to see the opening.

SECOND FLOOR

The collection starts in chronological order on the second floor, which covers Italian Primitives, Gothic, Renaissance and Baroque masterpieces spanning the 13th–17th centuries.

The collection of Gothic painting **[2]** includes eight bizarre, less than heavenly, depictions of saints by Gabriel Lalesskircher.

Hans Holbein the Younger's *Portrait of King Henry VIII* **[5]**, painted in 1534–36, is in many ways the definitive image of the larger-than-life English king and is quite rightly one of the cornerstones of the Thyssen-Bornemisza Collection. It exudes the king's strident, and domineering personality, and indeed his all-encompassing power.

The painting contrasts brilliantly with another work in the same room: Juan de Flandes' depiction of a shy and timid princess *Portrait of an Infanta*—the princess in question is thought to be Catherine of Aragon, Henry VIII's first wife.

Vittore Carpaccio's *Young Knight in a Landscape* from 1510 **[7]** was originally thought to be by Dürer and forged with his signature—it is certainly good enough to pass as the German master's work. Carpaccio's name was only discovered when the painting was restored in 1958.

MUSEO THYSSEN-BORNEMISZA
SECOND FLOOR

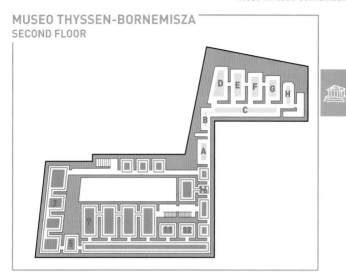

A classic Titian, *St Jerome in the Wilderness*—the hermit beating himself before the image of Christ—**[11]** dates from around 1575, painted shortly before the end of the artist's life when Titian was close on 90. This dark painting reflects the crisis in religion at the time.

On his travels local hero José de Ribera (internationally known as Jusepe de Ribera) absorbed several styles of European art—from the illuminist naturalism of Caravaggio, to the Venetian, Flemish and Renaissance movements—which all come together in the beautifully illuminated and coloured *Lamentation* **[12]**. Also in Room 12 hang several works by the much-imitated Caravaggio. The legendary artist called on a model for *St Catherine of Alexandria*, c. 1597—an actress who took centre stage in mystery plays in the palace of the Cardinal del Monte—to impart a greater sense of realism. The same model also sat for other works by Caravaggio, such as *Judith and Holofernes*, and *Mary Magdalene*.

FIRST FLOOR

The first floor includes 17th-century Dutch painting, with scenes of everyday life and landscapes, to the Neoclassicists, Impressionists, Fauves and the German Expressionists.

Edouard Manet's unfinished *Woman in a Riding Habit, Fullface*, c.1882 [32], belongs to his last creative push a year before his death, realising incredible new bounds between the application of light and colour.

Also in Room 32, Claude Monet's *The Thaw at Vétheuil* from 1881 comes from the artist's bleakest personal period when a cruelly ironic lack of sales had left him strapped for cash, and when he had only recently been made a widower, left distraught with two infants to bring up. The Seine—as so very often in Monet's paintings—is pictured here, though not this time in a warm and welcoming light, but with nature at its most cheerless, with a total absence of human interaction. This is one of 20 such works and is a masterpiece in the use of light, and of cold, lifeless colours.

Next door [33], Vincent van Gogh's 1888 creation *The Stevedores in Arles* comes from one of the great artist's most fruitful periods, and depicts a sunset with intense use of the colour orange contrasting superbly with dark silhouettes.

Next to it is *'Les Vessenots' in Auvers*, painted in 1890 not long before he took his own life in the village of Auvers-sur-Oise, where he spent the last two months of his life in a mental institution. Hardly depressing, with bright colours lighting up a non-oppressive scene, the flowing and ebbing brushstrokes nevertheless make what should be a comfortable setting harder to cope with—no doubt reflecting van Gogh's troubled mind.

Room 33 also features more post-Impressionism from Gauguin, Dégas and Cézanne, with a solitary work by the distinctive Toulouse Lautrec. The next room [34] features Fauves, such as Raoul Dufy, Robert Delaunay and Henri Martin.

Following this the display gives a very detailed history of the entire movement of Expressionism [35–40]. Kirchner, Kandinsky and Beckmann are all represented, including the latter's classic *Quappi in a Pink Jumper*, dated 1932–34, a portrait of his second wife.

MUSEO THYSSEN-BORNEMISZA
FIRST FLOOR

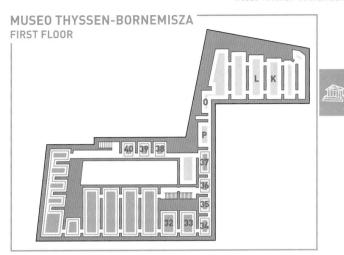

George Grosz, one of the founders of the Dada movement in Berlin in 1918, had to put aside the painting of *Metropolis—View of the Metropolis* **[40]** when he was drafted into the German army in the First World War. This landmark work was left unfinished as the fledgling artist was almost shot after a court marshal for insubordination. Grosz's hatred of authority and anarchistic tendencies come to the fore in this Cubist-influenced, Futurist-cum-Expressionist vision of hard-edged city life. The painting was unsurprisingly seized and dubbed degenerate by the Nazis.

GROUND FLOOR
The collection winds down with the experimental avant-gardes: Neo-Plasticism, Cubism, Dada, Surrealism, and Pop Art amongst others.

Of the very early Cubist works, the portrayal of the subject from several viewpoints and departure from two-dimensional forms, as developed by Pablo Picasso and Georges Braque between 1907 and 1914, are Picasso's *Still Life: Glasses and Fruit* and Braque's *Woman with a Mandolin* [41]. Also in Room 41 is Picasso's *Man with a Clarinet* (1911–12) is a more mature work from the genre.

The colourful, grid-like *New York City* by Piet Mondrian [43], painted between 1940–1942, is actually an unfinished work though reveals much of the artist's use of various genres from Fauvism, Expressionism, Cubism and Abstraction to create something that is indisputably Mondrian. His abstract *Grey-Blue Composition*, dated 1912-1913 is in the adjacent room [44].

Mark Rothko's *Green on Maroon* [46] was painted in 1961, the same year that New York's Museum of Modern Art ran a major exhibition on his work—which did nothing to lift the great North American Abstract Expressionist's lingering depression. This can be clearly seen in the limited and gloomy colours contained within just a couple of rectangular shapes.

Pop Art, Surrealism and Figurative Art, including Salvador Dalí, are well represented [47–48]. In Room 48 is Pop Artist Robert

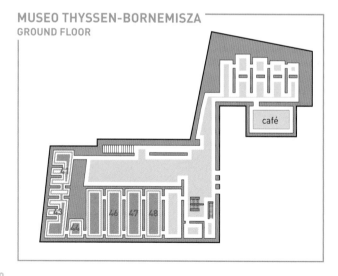

MUSEO THYSSEN-BORNEMISZA
GROUND FLOOR

café

41

44 46 47 48

Rauschenberg's *Express 1963*. The room as a whole is a veritable melange of different contributions avant-garde styles.

In the same room is *Woman in a Bath*, Roy Lichtenstein's 1963 Pop Art classic of mid-20th-century consumer society, with its comic-like imagery; and Ronald B. Kitaj's *Smyrna Greek (Nicos)*—in which the painter himself is pictured exiting a brothel as the poet Constantine Cavafys remains oblivious to a prostitute's advances.

THE CARMEN THYSSEN-BORNEMISZA COLLECTION

HIGHLIGHTS

The Garden Of Eden – **Jan Brueghel**

The Lock – **Constable**

Charing Cross Bridge – **Monet**

The Harvesters – **Picasso**

Seated Woman – **Juan Gris**

The Ludwigskirche in Munich – **Kandinsky**

The chronological route around the new rooms starts next to Room 18 of the Thyssen-Bornemisza collection (second floor; *plan on p. 37*).

17th-century painting from the likes of Jan Brueghel, van Dyck and Luca Giordano is well represented **[A–B]**. Room A covers the move to subject paintings of the Italian Baroque, including the *Return from the Flight into Egypt* by Romanelli, *Venus and Mars* by Annibale Carracci and Luca Giordano's Caravaggio-influenced epic *Judgment of Solomon*.

Flemish landscapes—*The Garden of Eden* by Jan Brueghel with landscapes from van der Neer, van Ruysdael, van Goyen and Verhaecht—are the focus of Room B. There are also paintings of everyday Dutch life, by Jacobus Vrel and de Hooch.

Paul Gauguin: *Mata Mua* (1892)

Van Dyck's resplendent *Christ on the Cross* is the gallery's sole religious work.

The long gallery [C] chronicles landscape painting over four centuries, including Canaletto's *Porta Portello, Padua*, Constable's *The Lock* and Vincent van Gogh's *Watermill at Gennep*, while a smaller room leading off it [D] focuses on French and Italian works of the 18th century.

After that comes 19th-century North American painting [E–F], with landscapes from Frederic Edwin Church, Albert Bierstadt, William Louis Sontag, Martin Johnson Heade and Sandford Robinson Gifford. There are also genre pieces, such as *Children on the Beach* by Samuel S. Carr, and the *The Local Bully* and *Tough Customers* from John George Brown.

Naturalism and the rural environment is also covered [G], with work from the French Barbizon School and the Dutch Hague School.

Early Impressionism is the focus of the final room [H], with works from the participants of the landmark 1874 Paris exhibition. Pioneering works in the dramatic and spontaneous use of light come from Dégas, Pissarro, Monet, Renoir and Sisley amongst others.

The French Impressionist movement is broken up by marble sculptures from Rodin in Room I and on the main staircase, and by American Impressionists who for the most part learnt their trade in Europe, including Hassam, Twachtman, Frieseke, Metcalf and Sargent.

The first-floor collection (*plan on p. 39*) takes us to Late Impressionism from Gauguin, Monet, Pissarro, Sisley, Gillaumin, Maximilien Luce, Berthe Morisot and Spain's own Joaquín Sorolla [K]. Works include Monet's *Charing Cross Bridge*, Gauguin's *Market Garden below the Church at Bihorel*, Sisley's *Bend in the River Loing*, and *The Apple Tree* by Pissarro.

Famous works by Gauguin are *Allées y Venues*, *Martinique* and *Mata Mua* [L].

The collection contains plenty of examples of the powerful,

colourful and free expression of Fauvism [O], which was led by Matisse, and includes his *The Midi Canal*, *Harbour at L'Estaque* by Braque, and *Landscape near Chattou* by Derain. There are also works exhibited by Max Beckmann, Vlaminck and Manguin.

Next door [P] are the early avant-gardes, encompassing Cubism and Orphism, as certain artists moved beyond the realm of imitation to more elaborate forms of representation.

Exhibits include Picasso's *The Harvesters* from 1907, *Seated Woman* by Madrid's own Juan Gris, *Portuguese Woman—La grande Portuguese* by Robert Delaunay, *The Bridge* by Fernand Léger and *Still Life with Bananas* by Raoul Dufy.

Parque del Buen Retiro

The green and watery expanse of the Retiro is a fine place to wind down after taking in an overdose of the outstanding paintings on show nearby; a place where the pace of adrenalin-rush Madrid noticeably slows. The centrepiece, Alfonso XII's imposing mausoleum, designed by José Grases Riera and completed in 1922, looks out onto a lake on which the boats can be hired all year round. There's also a sphinx-laden Egyptian fountain, and the attractive Puerta de la Independencia, which forms the entry point from the Calle de Alcalá.

Just to remind you that you're in a major art centre, the park boasts some outstanding exhibition spaces. The Palacio de Cristal is a superb venue for displaying surreal works, and is used by the Reina Sofía, as is the Palacio de Velázquez. The Casa de Vacas is also a prominent art venue hosting temporary exhibitions. Retiro also has an attractive rose garden, La Rosaleda, designed by Cecilio Rodríguez, and in the summer there are puppet shows for children, as well as a plethora of buskers and even tarot-card readers.

SYMPATHY FOR THE DEVIL

There are not many parks where you'll find a statue of Lucifer, and the Monumento al Ángel Caído is quite possibly the only one of its kind. Built by Ricardo Bellver in 1878, El Ángel Caído, the fallen angel, looks aghast and indignant, and particularly amusing are the snide and grotesque little devils spouting water into the fountain. **M** Banco de España. (This is better than Retiro, as the station bearing the park's name is separated from the park by the six-lane Calle de Alcalá, which you shouldn't even attempt to cross.)

REAL JARDÍN BOTÁNICO

Plaza de Murillo 2, T 91 420 3017. Open 10am–sunset Oct–April and until 9pm for the rest of the year. Closed 25/12, 1/1. Admission: €2; students €1; seniors and children free.

The Royal Botanic Garden is located directly opposite the back entrance of the Prado. The entrance is flanked by fine Neoclassical columns built by Juan de Villanueva (architect of the Prado) in 1789, which give way to 20 sumptuous acres of plant life and over 30,000 species.

   The foundation of the Royal Botanic Garden of Madrid was decreed by King Fernando VI in 1755 and, in the reign of Carlos III, the garden was moved from the banks of the Manzanares to its present location on the Paseo del Prado. Architect Francesco Sabatini (who built the Reina Sofía) started the plans off, but was replaced by Villanueva, who worked with botanist Casimiro Gómez Ortega in creating a research centre.

   From the outset, the aim of the garden was not only to exhibit plants, but to cultivate exotic species and classify new species originating from Spain's many colonies. It has also served as a source of medical supplies. The garden to this day houses an important botanical research centre. A very nice place to escape the crowds. **M** Atocha/Atocha Renfe

MUSEO NACIONAL DE ARTES DECORATIVAS

C/Montalbán 12, T 91 532 6845. Open 9:30am–3pm Tues–Sat, 9:30am–3pm Sun and holidays. Closed Mon. Admission €2.40, €1.20 discount. Sundays free.

Housed in a small late 19th-century palace, the National Museum of Decorative Arts hosts ceramics, decorations and furniture from

Monumento al Ángel Caído (1878)

the 15th to the 19th centuries. It provides a fascinating insight into Spanish interior decoration over the ages. It is especially notable for its 18th-century kitchen with 1,604 painted tiles (top floor). The tiles portray servants making a drink for the lady of the house, serving her cakes amid a backdrop of hanging meats, game, sausages and salted cod—rather like an upmarket tapas bar. The work was brought over tile by tile from its original Valencian home.

Ceramics also include collections from the Teruel and Talavera schools. There are also Flemish tapestries, Spanish carpets from the 15th and 16th centuries and decorative art items brought to Spain by the Bourbons. *M* Retiro

MUSEO DEL EJÉRCITO

C/Méndez Núñez 1, T 91 522 8977. Open 10am–2pm. Closed Mon. Admission €1, €0.50 discount. Saturdays free.

NB: At the time of writing this terrific collection of military regalia and memorabilia was expected to be moved to Toledo, to make way for the Prado extension.

The Sala de Heroinas is dedicated to women and their role in war, and includes a portrait of Manuela Malasaña, heroine of the infamous Dos de Mayo uprising against the French (*see p. 82*), who died in the fighting. The neighbourhood in which this seamstress rallied the locals against their despised occupiers is named after her (*see p. 104*).

The Sala de la Guerra Civil (the Civil War) contains the chair used by General Franco in his office in Burgos, and a reproduction of General Moscardo's office in Toledo. Moscardo and his nationalist soldiers held out under siege in Toledo's Alcázar for two months against Republican Militia. *M* Retiro/Banco de España

Museo de la Real Academia de Bellas Artes de San Fernando

OPEN	Tues–Fri 9am–7pm. Sat, Sun, Mon, and holidays. 9am–2.30pm
CHARGES	€2.40/€1.20 free Weds
TELEPHONE	91 522 00 46.
WEB	rabasf.insde.es (Spanish only)
MAIN ENTRANCE	C/Alcalá 13
DISABLED ACCESS	No
METRO	Sevilla/Sol
SERVICES	Tiny shop

HIGHLIGHTS

Works by Goya

Somewhat thrown together, not unlike Madrid itself, the Real Academia de San Fernando is a jumble of some excellent pieces of art from the 16th century to the present. A fair share of the works were donated by fledgling artists trying to paint their way in, from those employed there or those working in Madrid at the time. Don't expect to see anything by Dalí, however: he was expelled from the academy after a couple of bust-ups with his lecturers over 'artistic differences' (*see box on p. 50*).

Created in 1774, the Royal Academy of San Fernando, housed in the 17th-century Baroque palace of Juan de Goyeneche, is the oldest art institute in Madrid, and quite probably the oldest in all Spain. It's something like a Prado in miniature, with its focus on works by Spanish, Flemish, and Italian artists. You can see masterpieces by El Greco, Rubens, Velázquez, Zurbarán, Ribera, Cano, Coello, Murillo, Goya and Sorolla. The collection—which was started in 1752 during the reign of Fernando VI—has more than 1,500 paintings and 570 sculptures, ranging from the 16th century to the present.

This museum is a somewhat tricky to navigate, with no floor plan available, and room numbers which are surprisingly unintuitive. To cut straight to the gems, as you go upstairs to the permanent exhibition turn left to the entrance. On going in, we suggest starting with the room to the right, which has some excellent Goyas. His *Casa de Locos* ('Madhouse') with its sprawled naked bodies, each locked in their own unhinged world, oblivious to their surroundings and to their fellow inmates, is particularly moving. One poor deluded soul in the bottom right seems to think he's a king. Goya was later to become a master of portraying madness, in the paintings of his dark period, as foreshadowed also in the *Burial of the Sardine*.

The following room is mostly given over to Goya portraits, where the trademark dark background, which serves to highlight the model and especially the face, is very much in evidence. A much contrasting and classical style can be seen in self-portrait by Bayeu, Goya's brother-in-law, who helped further the young Goya's career.

There's also a Goya self-portrait from 1815 and one of Juan de Villanueva, who built the Prado.

The third and following room contains impressive works, such as Giuseppe Arcimboldo's *Spring*, a very early surrealistic piece that dates back to c. 1563. There are also Rubens's *Susanna and the Elders*, Jordaens' *Diana en Castillo*, plus paintings by van Dyck and Jans Jannsen.

In the fourth room Murillo's *La Magdalena* from c. 1650 has the classic blackened out background with just her face, shoulders, neck and praying hands emphasised by his dramatic use of light. There are also a couple of small but characteristic portraits by Velázquez—an addled Felipe IV and Mariana of Austria. Zurbarán's portraits of monks clad in long white gowns are followed by a couple of El Grecos.

On the next floor, currently off limits until further notice, the San Fernando also has works by Sorolla, Vicente López and Picasso.

Cheeky young upstarts

Two of the academy's most famous pupils, none other than Pablo Picasso and Salvador Dalí, could hardly be said to have been model students of the San Fernando—for what seemed to be the awful artistic sin of being a bit too cocky.

Picasso attended during the winter semester of 1896–97 (he was 16), but soon had his fill of being lectured and decided to go it alone. All in all he didn't spend much time in the capital. During his second stint in Madrid, aged 20, his friend Casagemas committed suicide in Paris, which led to Picasso taking over his friend's studio and uprooting from Spain altogether.

For Dalí, it was in while studying in Madrid at the San Fernando in the early 1920s that he met the legendary writer Federico García Lorca and the equally legendary film director Luis Buñuel. Whether due to the influence of his lofty companions or just plainly because he was one step ahead of his lecturers, Dalí was sent packing on the charge of inciting a student rebellion after criticising his lectures in 1923. He went back to the academy in 1925, only to be expelled again for refusing to take his final examination, arguing that he knew more than the examiner.

Picasso (with Braque) went on to develop Cubism a decade after leaving San Fernando, and Dalí went almost straight in to creating some ground-breaking Surrealist works. Which all goes to show that an education isn't everything.

in the area

Banco de España *C/Alcalá 48, T 913 385 000.* The Bank of Spain has a formidable art collection, including two Goya portraits. However, you'll need to apply in writing a long time in advance of your trip to secure permission to see it. Contact: Banco de España, Alcalá 48, 28014 Madrid. *M* Banco de España **Map p. 8, A3**

Barrio de los Jerónimos This plush and peaceful residential area tucked away between the Prado and the Retiro is, not surprisingly, one of the city's most coveted and expensive. You might recognise it from Pedro Almodóvar's film *Women on the Verge of a Nervous Breakdown*, which was set in an apartment in the area. *M* Atocha **Map p. 8, B4–C4**

Casa de Lope de Vega *C/Cervantes 11, T 91 429 9216. Tues–Fri 9.30am–2pm, Sat 10am–noon. Admission €2, €1 concession.* The great Spanish playwright, equally prolific with the ladies as with his output of dramas, lived here for a quarter of a century until his death in 1635. He wrote 1,500 plays in all, and while there's no record of his female conquests, he did have a marked liking for leading actresses. Not many of his possessions have survived the passage of time, though this is a highly credible recreation of a 17th-century Madrid house. Lope de Vega finally settled here with Marta de Nevares Santoyo, and it is here that he produced some of his most distinguished works, such as *Peribáñez*, *Fuente Ovejuna*, *El Caballero de Olmedo* and *El Castigo sin Venganza*. The street is named after another—more famous—author, who some say died at no. 2. *M* Antón Martín **Map p. 8, B3**

La Cuesta de Moyano *C/Claudio Moyano.* Engaging permanent book fair consisting of up to 30 book stalls that have been opening every day since 1925, when the mayor of Madrid, Count Vallellano, decided to bring the city's disparate book stalls together in one place. Just the place to rummage around in search of that elusive book that can't be traced elsewhere. Everything from Harold Robbins paperbacks to serious collectors' items. La Cuesta is at its busiest on Sundays, though quite a few stalls are open every day. *M* Atocha **Map p. 8, C4**

El Congreso de los Diputados *Carrera de San Jerónimo s/n. Open to the public on public holidays when queues go right around the corner and past the entrance of the Thyssen. Guided tours on Saturday mornings from 10 am–1pm. To book, T 91 390 6750.* Home to the Cortes, or the Spanish Parliament, where politicians have been meeting since 1830. The building is notable for its giant Corinthian columns, designed by Giuseppe Pagniucci and executed by a team of Italian sculptors. The pediment is adorned by allegorical sculptures by Ponciano Ponzano, who also created the two lions on the steps. The Catalan architects Clos, Rubery de Ventos and Parcerisa put in the glass extension in 1990, amid a not insignificant amount of protest.

A statue of Miguel de Cervantes by Antonio Sola has stood since 1835 in the triangular Plaza de las Cortes. *M* Sevilla **Map p. 8, B3**

Estación de Atocha Atocha railway station's tropical gardens, like a mini rainforest in the middle of the urban jungle, are a far better place to wait for a train than any waiting room you'll ever encounter. It's definitely worth a look, just for a breath of oxygen, even if you're not travelling anywhere. *M* Atocha **Map p. 8, D4**

Museo Nacional de Antropología *C/Alfonso XII, Open Tues–Fri 10.30am–7.30pm, Sun 10am–2pm. Admission €2.40, free all day Sun and Sat after 2.30pm.* Spain's National Museum of Anthropology was founded by the more than eccentric surgeon and scientist Dr Pedro González Velasco, who on losing his cherished teenage daughter supposedly had her body embalmed, and even took her out for rides in his carriage, as if she were still alive.

The collection, as might be expected, is a medley of curious and macabre exhibits, culled from Velasco's and others' travels, and include the skeleton of the 28-year-old latter-day serial killer Juan Tomás Blanco, a giant's skeleton and mummies of Gaunches, who were the original inhabitants of the Canary Islands.

The museum itself, with its columned Neoclassical entrance, was designed by Marqués de Cubas in 1873. *M* Atocha **Map p. 8, D4**

The palm-filled Estación de Atocha

Museo Naval *Paseo del Prado 5, T 91 379 5299. Tues–Sun 10am–2pm. Free admission.* All you need to know on Spain's great relationship with the seas and the battles it has fought on them. Not to be missed is Juan de la Cosa's map of the territories of the New World displayed in the room devoted to the Discovery of America; the first of its kind. 17th-century globes by Coronelli are also eye-catching. Look out also for the Nazi flag that once hung from the German warship *Deutschland*, which took a battering from Republican planes off the coast of Ibiza in 1937. *M* Banco de España **Map p. 8, B4**

Plaza de la Cibeles An amazingly ornate roundabout, in the middle of which the enchanting fountain of Cybele, the mother goddess of the ancient Phrygians, demands to be looked at. She is flanked by some incredible architecture too, most notably the Palacio de Comunicaciones (*see p. 143*). Although a defining symbol of Madrid, the fountain—designed by Ventura Rodríguez and José Hermosilla—takes its fair share of abuse from football fans celebrating Real Madrid's successes, of which there have been many. *M* Banco de España **Map p. 8, A4**

Plaza de Neptuno The square which divides the Prado from the Thyssen and the Ritz hotel from the Palace takes its popular name from the imposing statue of the sea god. Its real name is actually Plaza de Cánovas del Castillo. The fountain commemorates Spain's dominance of the seas and its colonial successes, and was sculpted by Juan Pascual de Mena and José Rodríguez from designs by Ventura Rodríguez. While Real Madrid fans celebrate their victories at Plaza de la Cibeles (*see above*), Neptuno is mobbed by supporters of Atlético Madrid (on the occasion that they actually win something). *M* Banco de España **Map p. 8, B3**

Real Fábrica de Tapices *C/Fuenterrabía 2, Mon–Fri 10am–2pm, Admission €2.50. T 91 434 0550, www.realfatapices.com* Founded by Felipe V in 1721 to provide tapestry fit for a king, this still-functioning workshop churns out elaborate and magnificent designs from cartoons by Goya amongst others. It designs, weaves and repairs tapestry and is more than prepared to adapt to modern tastes—which is probably why it's been open so long. High-paying clients have included the nearby Ritz and the Spanish royal family. *M* Menéndez Pelayo/Atocha Renfe **Map p. 9, D2**

commercial galleries

Helga de Alvear *C/Doctor Fourquet 12, T 91 468 05 06.* Continues the legacy of interest in avant-garde styles begun by the Galería Juan Mordó (1964–1995), focusing in recent years on photography, video, and installations, as well as other idioms used by conceptual and minimalist artists. Artists represented include Adolfo Schloser, Hannah Collins and Javier Vallhonrat. *M* Atocha **Map p. 8, D3**

Galería & Ediciones Ginkgo *C/Doctor Fourquet 6, T 91 539 92 52. Open 5–9 every evening.* Pint-sized gallery with graphic art from artists including Mitso Miura, Eva Lootz and Adolfo Schloser. *M* Atocha **Map p. 8, D2**

Galería Mouiren *C/Prado 12, T 91 420 0409.* Frenchman Jean Mouiren's new gallery, in which he indulges his love of painting bullfighters and other classics of the Spanish south. *M* Antón Martín **Map p. 8, B2**

Cruce *C/Argumosa 28, T 91 528 77 83.* New kid on the block exhibiting works from up-and-coming artists. They also hold lectures and conferences. *M* Atocha **Map p. 8, D3**

EFTI *C/Fuenterrabía 4–6, T 91 552 9999.* Combined photography school and exhibition space as well as host of the Hoffman Prize, top accolade for upcoming young photographers. Exhibitors include photographer Isabel Muñoz. Also looks at art and its impact on the commercial sphere. *M* Atocha Renfe **Map p. 9, D2**

Galería Leandro Navarro *C/Amor de Dios 1, T 91 4298955.* Promotes contemporary Spanish painters and sculptors. You can also catch works by the ever popular El Paso group (who are exhibited in the Reina Sofía) and the so-called Madrid School. It's also big on very famous names: Picasso, María Blanchard, Gutiérrez Solana and Zuloaga) and post-Civil War Realism, Informalism and abstract art by Millares, Lucio Muñoz, Feito and Saura. *M* Antón Martín **Map p. 8, C2**

Window in Lavapiés

eat

Unless otherwise stated restaurants are open 1pm—4pm and 9pm— midnight.

RESTAURANTS

€€€ Goya Restaurant *Hotel Ritz. Plaza de la Lealtad 5, T 91 701 6767.* Long considered a bastion of old-world splendour, the Ritz is adapting to modern demands, especially when it comes to dining. Chef Jorge González, who was poached from the Wellington Hotel, is producing some highly innovative dishes that use the best international ingredients and touches to enhance Mediterranean and Spanish classics. Javier Gila, one of Spain's top sommeliers, is on hand to guide you through the comprehensive wine list. While naturally expensive, the Sunday Brunch is €65 per person plus VAT, though children under 12 are served free and a set lunch menu is €48 plus VAT. Breakfast menus are also served and there's a lovely terrace restaurant in summer. NB: Jacket required. *M* Banco de España **Map p. 8, B4**

Lhardy *Carrera de San Jerónimo 8, T 91 522 2207.* Founded by Emile Lhardy in 1839, taking up *Carmen* author Prosper Mérimée's challenge to establish a top-class restaurant in Madrid. And this is indeed one of Madrid's top restaurants—with very top prices. Downstairs is a haven of gourmet tapas that won't wound your wallet. *M* Sevilla/Sol **Map p. 8, B2**

€€ El Bilbaíno *C/Ventura de la Vega 11, T 91 531 0094.* A vast range of dishes from the middle and northern reaches of the country. Good prices in an expensive area. *M* Sevilla **Map p. 8, B2**

Café del Príncipe *Plaza Canalejas 5, T 91 5318 183.* There's a bar downstairs and a fairly classy restaurant upstairs with a low-priced daily menu. A fine vantage point from which to view the swarming masses passing below. *M* Sol/Sevilla **Map p. 8, B2**

El Cenador del Prado *C/Prado 4, T 91 429 1561.* Creative dishes from chef Tomás Herranz, Spanish at the core with a French and Asian veneer in a stylish Baroque setting. Specialities include *solomillo sobre hojaldre a la pera* (fillet of veal on fruit pastry), and *patatas a la importancia* (sliced potatoes fried in a sauce of garlic, parsley, and clams). Expensive, though much more affordable at lunchtime with its daily menus of around €25, for which politicians and civil servants from the nearby Cortes flock in. Extensive wine list. **M** Antón Martín **Map p. 8, B2**

Don Paco *C/Caballero de Gracia 36, T 91 531 4480.* Welcoming restaurant with the lure of the Spanish south, said to be the oldest Andalucian restaurant in Madrid. Popular dishes include *tortillitas de camarones*, *huevas aliñadas* and *boquerones victorianos*. Sweetbreads in sherry are another delicacy. **M** Gran Vía **Map p. 8, A2**

La Paella de la Reina *C/Reina 39, T 91 531 1885.* Nothing flash about the restaurant itself, La Paella de la Reina lets its paellas do the talking, whether they be dotted with seafood, or chicken and rabbit for landlubbers. Another favourite is *fideuà*, a paella made from noodles with squid. For more paella, compare and contrast with Restaurante La Barraca (*T 91 532 7154; Calle de la Reina 29, map p. 8, A2*). The conclusion is that competition is healthy. **M** Chueca **Map p. 8, A2**

Kupela *C/Marqués de Cubas 8, T 90 228 2028. Closed Sun.* Classy Basque eatery and cider house with dishes made from only the finest of northern ingredients to a backdrop of cider barrels and paintings of green Basque scenery. Kupela's forte is grilled meat dishes and monkfish and cod simmered in garlic *al pil pil*. Tucked away behind the Parliament and the Thyssen. Booking recommended. **M** Banco de España **Map p. 8, B3**

€ **Do Salmon** *C/León 4, T 91 429 3952.* Good value, no-nonsense Galician restaurant serving plenty of tasty fish dishes: *merluza* (hake) *a la gallego*, *bonito* (tuna) *con tomate* and, as its name would suggest, salmon. The piping hot *caldo gallego* is just the broth to warm the cockles on a chilly day. Washed down with white Galician wines and reds from the warmer climes of Spain. Great value *menú del día* for €10, though inexpensive à la carte also. **M** Antón Martín **Map p. 8, C2**

La Finca de Susana *C/Arlabán 4, T 91 369 3557.* Superb value for creative cuisine, attracting hungry people from all walks of life. It can be difficult to get your foot in the door of this incredibly popular restaurant, though. Best get there as soon as it opens (1 pm) or face a long wait. **M** Sevilla **Map p. 8, B2**

La Gloria de Montera *C/Caballero de Gracia 10, T 91 523 4407.* Just as difficult to get a table as at its sister restaurant the Finca de Susana (*see above*), La Gloria de Montera excels in creative

Mediterranean dishes in a cool contemporary setting. Great value daily menu. No booking so get there early or join the hungry queue. *M* Gran Vía **Map p. 8, A2**

La Pepa 1812 *C/Zorrilla 7, T 91 429 6258*. Tucked away in no-man's-land between Huertas and Gran Vía, in a building constructed in 1812, this is a modern but cosy and welcoming establishment. A *menú del día* takes in various specialities from around the country, and the focus is more on presentation rather than on big helpings. *M* Sevilla **Map p. 8, B3**

Rillón *C/Ave María 29, T 91 528 2490*. Cracking value eatery serving up decent Spanish standards. *Menú de la casa* from €6.30 and a *menú del día* for €7.30. *M* Lavapiés **Map p. 8, C2**

OTHER CUISINES

€€ **El Inti de Oro** *C/Ventura de la Vega 12, T 91 429 6703*. Highly rated Peruvian restaurant. A daily menu for €18 offers a decent introduction. *M* Sevilla **Map p. 8, B2**

Wokcafé *C/Infantas 44, T 91 522 90 69. Open from 9am 'til late*. Much more stylish than its cuisine is authentically Asian, the Wokcafé continues to pack 'em in. Though very close to the museum area, Wokcafé definitely belongs to Madrid's funky Chueca district. The offering includes some very westernised-sounding offerings as well as loads of noodles and rice dishes, with sushi making an appearance too. Also does breakfasts. *M* Gran Vía **Map p. 8, A3**

€ **Taj Indian Restaurant** *C/Marqués de Cubas 6, T 91 531 5059. Open every day 1pm–4pm and 8.30pm–11.30pm*. Popular Indian restaurant offering good value, filling weekday menus for €10.95 (very good Nan bread—they ask you how spicy you want it). Extensive list of à la carte fare. There's a sister restaurant at *C/de la Cruz 13, T 91 531 5059 (map p. 8, B2)*. *M* Banco de España **Map p. 8, B3**

VEGETARIAN

Al Natural *C/Zorrilla 11, T 91 369 4709*. One of the ever-proliferating veggie places in the city. Takes the meat out of many classically-named non-veggie dishes, but retains plenty of oomph. Right behind the Parliament. *M* Sevilla **Map p. 8, B3**

Elfindelafán *C/Núñez de Arce 4, T 91 360 4528*. Vegetarian café bar in chilled-out setting with veggie pies, freshly squeezed juices and the like. *M* Sevilla/Sol **Map p. 8, B2**

BARS & TAPAS

Las Bravas *C/Álvarez Gato 3, T 91 532 2620.* Incredibly this place has patented the sauce for its *patatas bravas.* It also has many other types of tapas on offer. It's a bit McDonalds in its approach, but they do do their own version of *orejas,* another Madrid classic. More branches around town too. *M* Sol **Map p. 8, B2**

El Brillante *C/Doctor Drumén 7, T 91 528 6966. Open 6.30am–12.30am.* Large, walk-through snack and tapas joint right next to the Reina Sofía. A good place to grab some typical Spanish scran between museum visits or to start the day, whether for breakfast on the way to the Reina Sofía, or before taking a train out from Atocha—or more likely on the way home after a night of revelling. *M* Atocha **Map p. 8, C4**

Café Melo's *C/Ave María 44, T 91 527 5054.* It's fascinating to watch the speed with which the lady of the house assembles and prepares the quality tapas on offer here. She seems to have a hand in every part of the process, down to slapping the cheese and ham on the grill for the very tasty *zapatillas*—it means 'small shoes', though these are actually very large sandwiches. The *pimientos de padrón* are bursting in flavour, as are freshly rolled and deep fried *croquetas.* Galician run. *M* Lavapiés **Map p. 8, C2**

Candela *C/Olmo 2, T 91 467 3382.* Squeeze your way into this immensely popular and genuine Flamenco place with a real late-night buzz about it. Live Flamenco blares out on loudspeakers from concerts taking place downstairs. You'll need to be connected to actually get downstairs, but never mind if you aren't—this is still a happening place. *M* Antón Martín/Lavapiés **Map p. 8, C2**

Casa del Abuelo *C/Victoria 12.* Steeped in atmosphere, decorated with tiles, and with prawn heads strewn over the floor: a gem of Spanish culture slap bang in the middle of the city's most touristic neighbourhood. Full-bodied sweet red wine from Valencia accompanies prawns that come either in garlic, or are charred on the grill. On paying, the barman might give you a voucher for a free drink at the sibling El Abuelo located just around the corner. The newer El Abuelo is a more relaxed affair, and serves a range of tapas with very tasty *patatas bravas,* cooked just to perfection. *M* Sol **Map p. 8, B2**

Casa Alberto *C/Huertas 18, T 91 429 9356.* Soaked in tradition—not surprising as it opened for business in 1827—with the trademark old zinc and marble bar, bullfighting memorabilia and paintings.

Seafood tapas are a speciality, though the snails and *chorizo* in cider sauce are particularly lush. There's a pleasant seating area at the back where you can sit down to lamb done in a variety of ways. *M* Antón Martín **Map p. 8, B2**

The Cock Bar *C/Reina 16, T 91 532 2826.* That's cock for cocktails! Has the feel of an English country club, which is quite an achievement in the middle of Madrid. It's a fine place to get the evening started with a gin and tonic or to wind down after dinner with one of the bar's famous cocktails. While it's not terribly formal, you might not get let in wearing trainers. *M* Gran Vía **Map p. 8, A2**

Los Gabrieles *C/Echegaray 17, T 91 360 0089.* The bar with the amazing tiles, which include a depiction of Velazquéz's *Los Borrachos* plus an imposing stuffed bull's head. Live Flamenco on Tuesdays and a variety of tracks spun otherwise. Things get a little messy later on in this former brothel. You might spot the occasional visiting film star. *M* Sevilla/Sol **Map p. 8, B2**

Matador *C/Cruz 39, T 91 531 8981.* Intimate and friendly drinks bar piled high with bric à brac all to the backing of a blaring flamenco soundtrack. *M* Sol **Map p. 8, B2**

El Mojito *C/Olmo 6, T 680 057844.* Cosy and intimate setting where cocktails are delicately made with the female touch as you try and remember what ingredients are going in. A number of Latin American cocktails are served—this is El Mojito after all. The hostess is also a painter, and her impressionist-cum-expressionist offerings are on display in the bar (and are reasonably priced). *M* Antón Martín/Lavapiés **Map p. 8, C2**

Museo del Jamón *Carrera de San Jerónimo 6, T 91 521 0346.* These jumbo ham expos, which you'll encounter all over town, are not the tourist traps you might expect. In fact as often as not, they are teeming with locals debating what makes a leg of ham truly special, or just hanging out for a quick snack. Some of the larger stores are quite spectacular, with literally hundreds of hams hanging from the ceiling, and are certainly worth a visit. They also serve the full gamut of alcoholic and soft drinks. Best not to take too long over your order if you can attract the barman's attention. Branches throughout Madrid. There's also a noteworthy variation on the tribute to *jamón* in the form of a rival chain: the slightly more laid back Palacios del Jamón, literally 'ham palaces'. *M* Sol **Map p. 8, B2**

La Oreja de Oro *C/Victoria 9*. Timeless classic with great tapas and tasty *pimientos del padrón*. You're quite likely to see a pig's head on a platter on the bar if you can get near it. The red wine's a bit like paint stripper while the slightly yeasty white wine comes in a mug that you might think is to clean your hands in—it all adds to the atmosphere. *M* Sol **Map p. 8, B2**

El Rinconcito *C/Espoz y Mina 28, T 639 682760*. Evenings only. Cheek-to-cheek late night bar just off the Plaza de Santa Ana run by charismatic and cosmopolitan Frenchman Walter Ferrari. A vast array of spirits and a solid choice of wines, served with tapas made from the classic Spanish ingredients, with a slightly different angle. French cheese sometimes, though Ferrari believes that Spanish cheese is almost in the same league. The *pièce de résistance*, though, are the cocktails. *M* Sol **Map p. 8, B2**

La Trucha *C/Manuel Fernández y González 3, T 91 429 5833*. A long-known bastion of fine tapas, 'the trout' is sticking to its guns when it comes to gourmet tapas, continuing to do what it always did well: fish done in the Andalucian style. Judging by the number of happy punters, it's doing just fine. This is one of those places where you pay more depending on where you sit. *M* Antón Martín/Sevilla **Map p. 8, B2**

Viva Madrid *C/Manuel Fernández y González 7, T 91 429 3640*. Gorgeous tiled bar, with a supreme ceiling. The ceiling doesn't come cheap, however, but no one minds about that: this is a classic Madrid establishment, and can get a bit overrun by night. Depending on your preference, you might find it at its best as a place for a sneaky drink early in the day, well before the madding crowds assemble. *M* Antón Martín/Sevilla **Map p. 8, B2**

CAFÉS

Bar La Piola *C/León 9, T 91 429 5544*. Café-cum-bar serving Italian coffee, and hosting exhibitions of sketches and paintings in all artistic styles. Exhibitions change monthly and prices for artworks average around €100. It's very easy to stretch out on its big comfy sofa. *M* Antón Martín **Map p. 8, B2**

Café Barbieri *C/Ave María 45, T 91 527 3658*. Spacious, softly lit and stylish though ever so slightly faded café, just up the road from Lavapiés metro station. Specialises in coffee, alcoholic coffees and cocktails. A mellow place to relax after dinner or just to get some respite from the frantic action outside. *M* Lavapiés **Map p. 8, C2**

Café del Círculo de Bellas Artes *C/Alcalá 42, T 91 521 6942.* A wonderful arty and spacious café to sit back and watch Madrid go by with artworks adorning the walls and a reclining nude sculpture stretching out in the middle of the floor. You'll need to buy your way in for one Euro, or sign up and become a member, though they don't levy any fee if you drop in for a spot of lunch. Offers two menus of substantial fare for its daily *menú*. *M* Banco de España **Map p. 8, A3**

El Económico *C/Argumosa 9, T 91 539 7371. Open from 9am–2am.* Nice relaxed spot for morning coffee and a read of the papers: the locals who come and go do the same, especially when the sun shines in on this wooden and tiled bar. Good value set lunches plus various tapas. *M* Lavapiés **Map p. 8, D2**

Salón del Prado *C/Prado 4, T 91 429 3361.* Classy and refined chandeliered coffee house, an ideal place to wile away the time over a long coffee or something stronger. Not as old as it might seem, this beautifully-lit venue opened as recently as 1984. It's the kind of place where they shoot scenes for the big screen. Often has live classic or a piano man tinkling away. For something to eat, check out the restaurant next door. *M* Sevilla **Map p. 8, B2**

WINE BARS

Casa Montes, *C/Lavapiés 40, T 91 527 0064.* Traditional and compact wine bar open since 1932 with bottles stacked efficiently and high to the ceiling behind the bar. Grab a couple of glasses and some tasty canapés and shuffle up to one of the barrels, which serve as makeshift tables, or else prop up the bar. To get to the toilet you'll have to limbo under the bar. Quite an experience. *M* Lavapiés **Map p. 8, C2**

Vinoteca Barbechera *C/Príncipe 27, T 91 420 0478.* Smart wine bar with a sophisticated older crowd, with Spanish and international wines available by the glass. Aram Cejudo Cueller oversees a venture that seeks to show the best of Spain's classic wines, while giving a fair share of the centre stage to wines from Spain's upcoming regions. *M* Sol/Antón Martín **Map p. 8, B2**

Vinitis *C/Ventura de la Vega 15, T 91 420 4090. Open 8pm–midnight in the week and later at weekends.* Relaxing, classy wine restaurant (you have to eat here as well as drink) with its offering racked up high. A wide choice of Spanish wines by glass and bottle, plus plenty of foreign vintages, including wines from Austria, Germany,

Portugal, New Zealand and Chile. It's €2 for a small glass of most of the wines, which keeps things simple. Dishes such as melted provolone cheese with dried Sicilian tomatoes, oxtail and tope stew with saffron and sherry match the wines amply. *M* Sevilla/Anton Martín **Map p. 8, B2**

shop

This is not the most densely concentrated area of Madrid for shops, but there are some old classics and a few trendy outfits that are certainly worth the time to explore. Note that many shops in Madrid, particularly the old-fashioned kind, take a siesta break until 5pm.

ACCESSORIES

ChG *C/Lope de Vega 12.* Snazzy and colourful bags in all the most eye-catching colours and materials. Also hats, T-shirts, gloves, earrings, jewellery and shawls. *M* Antón Martín **Map p. 8, B3**

Gil *Carrera de San Jerónimo 2.* Dates back to 1880, and it certainly feels like it when you step into this light-starved store that specialises in *mantoncillos* and *mantones*—those classic Spanish shawls that señoritas hardly seem to wear these days, though their grandmothers might. Also the place to get *mantillas*, traditional Spanish veils. *M* Sol **Map p. 8, B2**

ANTIQUES

Aurelio Ruiz Boillos *C/Prado 15.* Whopping chandeliers, 16th-century furniture and original paintings from across the centuries in these rich antique and art bonanzas. *M* Antón Martín **Map p. 8, B2**

CLOTHES

Capas Seseña *C/Cruz 23, T 91 531 6840.* Rumour has it that a handful of Spaniards really do wear capes in their free time. If you should happen to be looking for one—for whatever reason—this is most certainly the place. International celebrities seem to like them. *M* Sol **Map p. 8, B2**

Pepita is Dead *C/Doctor Fourquet 10. Closed 3 wks in August.* Perfect fashion store for retro clothing buffs, with stacks of clothes and accessories from the 60s, 70s and 80s—though absolutely none of it is second-hand. Seems they astutely snapped up what for years nobody else would touch with a bargepole. Good for them, as it's all somewhat in again. Summer, winter and party collections of all styles from those decades past, plus glasses, underwear, shoes, etc. Run by Cristina Guisado, whose own quirky clothes are also on offer. *M* Atocha **Map p.8, D3**

La Pintana *C/Lope de Vega 3.* Eclectic boutique with clothes from Okau, Lombok, Susymyped and Yokana, a wide variety of bags, decorations, jewellery and many odds and ends. *M* Antón Martín **Map p. 8, B3**

CRAFTS

La Casa Roja *C/Moratín 18.* Curious gift objects made from a variety of materials including crystal, clay, metal and leather. They also restore furniture and make jewellery. *M* Antón Martín **Map p. 8, C3**

Decodelia *C/Lope de Vega 26.* Lamps and furniture from the 50s, 60s and 70s by Óscar Tusquets, Pep Bonet, Miquel Milá. Also some distinctive jewellery on offer. *M* Antón Martín **Map p. 8, B3**

FOOD AND DRINK

Antigua Pastelería del Pozo *C/Pozo 8.* One of Madrid's superb old pastry shops, tucked away in a quiet spot in a frantic area. It actually began life as a straightforward baker (in 1830). *M* Sol **Map p. 8, B2**

La Casa del Bacalao *C/Carmen 26.* Cod galore in this exquisite little fishmonger that prepares this classic fish of the northern oceans—a key part of Spanish cuisine—in a variety of ways. The Spanish have combed distant waters for *bacalao* for centuries, hence the emphasis on salting and drying the fish, which despite the process retains its flavour and texture beautifully. Curiously, *bacalao* is also the name of a strain of techno dance music that hails from Valencia. *M* Sol/Gran Vía **Map p. 8, A1**

Casa Mira Turones *Carrera de San Jerónimo 28.* Beautiful and festive shop with it offerings of sweets and cakes of every description twirling temptingly around in the shop window. House made *turrón* is one of its specialities. *M* Sol/Sevilla **Map p. 8, B2**

González *C/León 12.* Cute, old-style delicatessen and wine shop-cum-tapas bar that's been selling its wares since 1931. *M* Antón Martín **Map p. 8, B2**

Licorilandia *C/León 30.* Curious liquor store that sells only miniature bottles of spirits. Ideal for mini gifts. *M* Antón Martín **Map p. 8, B2**

Maria Cabello *C/Echegaray 19.* Large choice of wines, sherries and spirits at all prices in intimate, old-style corner shop opened by Maria Cabello in 1913. *M* Sevilla **Map p. 8, B2**

FLORISTS

Martín Floristas *C/Huertas 2.* Open for over a century and still going strong. Just the place if you need to impress someone in a hurry. *M* Antón Martín **Map p. 8, B2**

INTERNET

Servicios Express Workcenter *C/Príncipe 1 (Plaza Canalejas).* Open all hours for checking emails, surfing the internet, making photocopies, etc. Branches around the city. *M* Sevilla/Sol **Map p. 8, B2**

JEWELLERY

Joyería García del Río *Carrera de San Jerónimo 30.* Classic traditional and Art Deco jewellery made from sterling silver. The business has been run by the same family since 1914. Also customised jewellery on request. *M* Sevilla/Sol **Map p. 8, B2**

MAPS

Amieva-México *C/Huertas 20.* Exquisite shop carrying antique maps of Madrid, the rest of the country and beyond. *M* Tirso de Molina/Antón Martín **Map p. 8, B2**

MUSIC

Unión Musical Española *Carrera de San Jerónimo 26.* Ornate and impressive two-level music store. Downstairs there's every type of rock instrument on display and Washburn guitars with Che Guevara plastered over them. Upstairs goes classical, stocking every instrument required for an orchestra. Sheet music galore. *M* Sevilla **Map p. 8, B2**

SHOES

Don Flamenco *C/León 26.* Colourful and striking flamenco shoes for women plus salon dancing shoes for men and women from this bijou shoemaking and repair outfit. Shoes come under such names as Dolores, Taranto, Fuego and Felino. *M* Antón Martín **Map p. 8, B2**

OLD MADRID

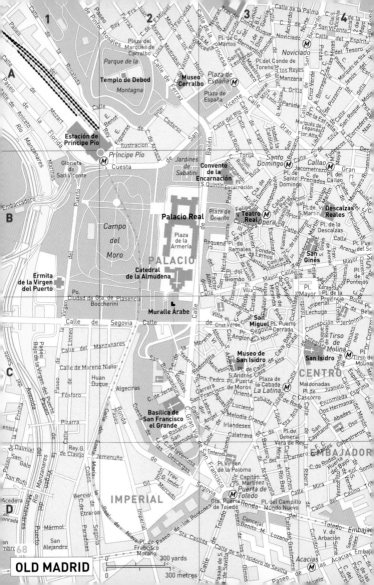

The winding streets of old Madrid are a joy to explore on foot, yielding surprises around every corner. With the sheer opulence of the Royal Place, the old town centres of Plaza Mayor and Sol, and the trendy hangout of La Latina with its gourmet tapas joints, this area exudes old Spain more than any other part of the city. Impressive architecture abounds, redolent of the imperial pomp of the Habsburg and Bourbon eras, and there is also a surviving smattering of earlier Moorish Madrid.

There are monasterial treasures to savour too, which offer peaceful sanctuary in the frenetic city. The area boasts a rich concentration of fine art plus more than its fair share of places to eat and shop.

There also vast areas of parkland, and fine squares onto which the chairs and tables pile out in the warmer months.

Palacio Real

OPEN	April 1–Sept 30 weekdays from 9am–6pm, holidays 9am–3pm; 1 October–31 March weekdays 9.30am–5pm, holidays 9am–2pm
CHARGES	€9; €3.50 reduced admission, free on Wednesdays to EU citizens. Closed 1/1, 6/1, 1/5, 15/5, 9/11, 25/12, 31/12
TELEPHONE	91 454 8800
ENTRANCE	C/Bailén
DISABLED ACCESS	Yes
METRO	Ópera
SERVICES	Shop

HIGHLIGHTS

Ceiling frescoes by Tiepolo and Mengs

Vicente López's *Allegory of the Foundation of the Order of Carlos III*

Goya: Royal Portraits

NB: The Royal Palace is no longer home to the Royal Family, who now reside in the less palatial Zarzuela Palace outside Madrid. The palace is used instead for various high level state functions and is often off-limits to the public, so it's a good idea to phone ahead and check. The parts open to the public are easy to navigate—keep looking up at the fabulous frescoes. To get a floorplan you have to pay for an audio guide (which provides a little too much detail for most). The information posted in each room is more than adequate.

Palacio Real

Madrid's Palacio Real, a powerhouse of Baroque architecture, stands on the site of Madrid's former Alcázar. The Muslim fortress was burnt to the ground in 1734, and Felipe V decreed that the palace of palaces was to go up in its place, though he didn't live to see the finished item. Felipe, the first of the Bourbon kings, hired Italian architect Filippo Juvarra (best known for his stupendous work for the Kings of Savoy in and around Turin). When Juvarra died in 1736, his fellow Italian Giovan Battista Sacchetti inherited the mantle, and completed the marvellously ornate, heavily Italian-influenced pile in 1764, during the reign of Carlos III, who in turn commissioned much of the decoration.

The palace is a spectacularly grand place to enter, and is ideal for impressing visitors. The long staircase is so well designed that you practically glide up it. Visitors have been many over the years. Passing through the Halberdiers' Hall [A] (which was used by the royal family's closest guards) with its military-themed ceiling fresco of *Vulcan forging arms for Aeneas* by Tiepolo, you come to the Hall of Columns [B], where the Middle East peace talks were held in 1992 and Spain's Treaty of Accession to what is now the European Union was signed in 1985. It was traditionally used as a reception room where the royals would get acquainted with commoners, washing the feet of 25 poorer subjects every Maundy Thursday.

The Throne Room [C], which is still used by the present king and queen to receive official guests, is splendidly overpowering with its red velvet walls, silver chandeliers, huge mirrors, and life-size bronze statues commandeered from Italy by Velázquez. All this is canopied by the *Apotheosis of the Spanish Monarchy*, the ceiling fresco painted by Tiepolo.

Carlos III took up residence in the next three rooms, often known as the Gasparini Rooms, after their original designer. It was in the Lounge [D] that Carlos III took luncheon. The room is decorated with four paintings by Luca Giordano, once court painter. Look up and you'll see the The *Apotheosis of Trajan* by Neoclassical master Anton Raphael Mengs, who also painted the *Apotheosis of Hercules* next door in the Antechamber [E]. The king

PALACIO REAL

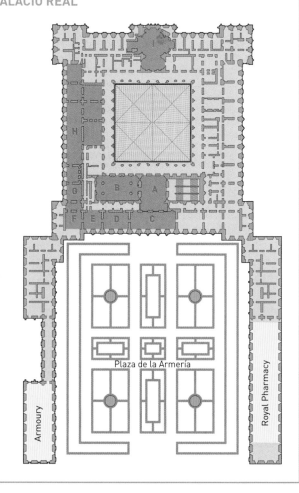

Plaza de la Armería

Armoury

Royal Pharmacy

is portrayed as a Greek colossus admirably and virtuously defending his empire. Four Goyas hang in the Antechamber: a pair of portraits of King Carlos IV and his wife Queen María Luisa of Bourbon-Parma. Keep an eye out too for the clock by Luis Godón, in which Time supports a celestial globe.

Carlos III's Chamber Room [F] is where the king held his private audiences. In Carlos III's Bedroom [G], where he passed away in 1788, Vicente López's *Allegory of the Foundation of the Order of Carlos III* is painted on the ceiling, and there is also a portrait of him by Mariano Salvador Maella, a Neoclassical painter and follower of Mengs.

The Gala Dining Room [H], completed in 1879 by King Alfonso XII, with its incredibly long dining table, is still used for official banquets. Diners are forcefully reminded of Spain's past glories as they are watched over by the epic fresco of *Columbus before the Catholic King and Queen* by Antonio G. Velázquez.

The Royal Chapel [I] was completed in 1757 by Ventura Rodríguez, who worked from Sacchetti's original designs. The

Chamber Room of Carlos III

ceiling fresco is by Giaquinto; and *St Michael* by Bayeu hangs above the high altar with Mengs' *Annunciation* over the side altar.

Coming out into the courtyard, the **Royal Pharmacy** can be found on the left. It looks like something straight out of Frankenstein's castle with its macabre-cum-fantasy mix of pestles, mortars, potions, jars and weird apparatus. The **Armoury** is also worth a look. El Cid's sword is to the left as you enter, and easily recognizable as it lost its handle. On the far side mounted is the suit of armour worn by King Carlos V in the famous Velázquez portrait housed in the Prado. There's even a suit of armour for some pampered pooch.

THE PALACE GROUNDS

Immediately adjoining the Royal Palace, a few steps along its eastern flank down C/de Bailén, you reach the pleasant Jardines de Sabatini, which was once the place where the royal stables stood. The gardens are a prelude to the Campo de Moro, the extensive former palace gardens. To get there, cross the Sabatini diagonally at the northwest corner and head left down Cuesta de San Vicente. Passing the attractive Estación del Príncipe Pío, you come to the gardens on the left. The almost English-style Campo de Moro takes its name from an unsuccessful siege carried out from here by the Moors in 1109.

The ever-busy architect Ventura Rodríguez (he has a metro station named after him) designed the fountain known as Fuente de las Conchas.

Heading west over the 'mighty' River Manzanares you come to a vast area of scrubland, the Casa de Campo, former hunting ground of Philip II (the man who launched the Armada, and later husband of Mary Tudor). In latter days it became notorious for hunting of another kind. Until the local authorities put the dampers on it in 2003, the Casa de Campo was a rampant prostitution zone and gay cruising spot. Now it is more of a place to take the kids—at least in the daytime.

The Parque de Atracciones amusement park (**M** Batán; beyond the map) offers a bunch of rides, various other attractions, restaurants, bars as well as a leisure area for kids. There's also a modern zoo, a large outdoor swimming pool, tennis courts and a boating lake. The Batán ranch rears bulls exclusively for the Fiestas de San Isidro.

Slightly north of the Campo de Moro is the pleasant Parque del Oeste (*map p. 102*). In this park, which is also shaking off its nocturnal reputation, the Teleférico de Madrid begins (T 91 541 7450, www.teleferico.com; Spanish only), a 2.5 km cable car ride that takes in the slopes of La Rosaleda and the Casa de Campo. *M* Argüelles

Monasterio de las Descalzas Reales

OPEN	Guided tours run 10.30am–12.45pm and 4pm–5.45pm Tues–Thurs and Sat, 11am–1.45pm on Sun and holidays
CHARGES	€5, €2.50 discount. Combined ticket with Convento de la Encarnación €6 (valid for 1 week). Free to EU citizens Wednesdays
TELEPHONE	91 454 88 00
WEB	www.patrimonionacional.es
ENTRANCE	Plaza de las Descalzas 3
DISABLED ACCESS	No
METRO	Callao/Sol/Ópera

HIGHLIGHTS

Floor-to-ceiling frescoes by José Ximénez Donoso, Claudio Coello, Francisco Rizzi and Dionisio Mantuano

Ship of Fools by an unnamed artist from the Bosch School

Recumbent Christ by Gaspar Becerra

Caesar's Coin by Titian

Offering welcome respite from the seething masses outside, the Royal Convent of the Barefoot Sisters is an oasis of calm, tranquillity and fine art just north of the bustling C/Arenal. Its unimpressive façade hides—even protects—the building's sumptuous interior from the outside world. The convent was set up in 1564 as a refuge for orphaned girls by Juana of Austria, daughter of Emperor Charles V and sister of Philip II, after she was widowed. Juana had been born here in 1535, and it was earlier home to the Emperor's treasurer Alonso Gutiérrez. Juan Bautista de Toledo, of El Escorial fame (*see p. 158*), oversaw the former palace's architectural transformation into a convent. The first nuns came over from Gandía on Spain's east coast, while many of the fantastic works of art came from aristocratic women who subsequently joined the convent.

The only way to see Descalzas Reales is to join one of the guided tours. Queues can be quite long, so either come early or wait. Tours are usually in Spanish and last slightly under an hour, though if English or German speakers are in the majority, the guides will switch to either of those languages. You could assemble enough English speakers from the queue to form a majority, though it hardly matters whether you can understand the guide: the convent is a feast for the eyes, and it's a more enjoyable experience to keep a few steps away from the herd. You can also ask the guide questions aside in English if you really feel the need. The tour takes you through the lower cloister to the kind of extravagant sight that you don't really expect to see in Madrid. Outlandish floor-to-ceiling frescoes by José Ximénez Donoso, Claudio Coello, Francisco Rizzi and Dionisio Mantuano adorn the grand staircase. They were not added until the end of the 17th century. All of this is proudly watched over by Felipe IV and family, seemingly welcoming visitors to the convent. The royal family and the cavalry are believed to have been painted by Antonio Pereda.

Up the staircase, 33 small but detailed chapels surround the upper cloister, each assigned to an individual nun to look after—

there are 33 nuns. The cloister itself was glassed over by Francesco Sabatini on the instructions of Carlos III in 1773. Look out for the recurring image of the infant Jesus resting on a skull, symbolising the triumph of eternal life over death. The stunning *Recumbent Christ* is by Gaspar Becerra, a follower of Michelangelo.

The upper cloister connects to the amazingly atmospheric Coro (choir), which houses the tomb of Empress María of Austria, who died in the convent. Juana of Austria is also buried in the convent. The sculpture *Virgen Dolorosa* by Pedro de la Mena, with tears pouring from its eyes, adds to the atmosphere.

Once the sleeping area of the nuns, the Tapestry Room has some intricate, lavish and grand 17th-century Flemish tapestries depicting the *Triumph of the Eucharist* from drawings by Rubens.

The convent has more than its fair share of excellent royal portraits and wooden sculptures which you are taken to now. Here you can take a peek out of the window at the convent's vegetable garden. Sometimes you can also hear the nuns tinkling away on the piano.

The Sala Flamenca holds some superb Flemish paintings, including the weird and wonderful *Ship of Fools* from a member of the Bosch school replete with demonic figures, an *Adoration of the Magi* by the elder Brueghel and one painting by Rubens. A *St Francis* attributed to Murillo and Titian's *Caesar's Coin* hang in the adjoining Sala Hispana-Italiana.

Convento de la Encarnación

OPEN — Guided tours run Tues–Thurs and Sat 10.30am–12.45pm and 4pm–5.45pm, Sun and holidays 11am–1.45pm

CHARGES — €3.60, €2 discount. Combined ticket with Convento de las

	Descalzas Reales €6 (valid for 1 week). Free to EU citizens Wednesdays
TELEPHONE	91 542 69 47
WEB	www.patrimonionacional.es/encarna
ENTRANCE	Plaza de la Encarnación
DISABLED ACCESS	No
METRO	Ópera

HIGHLIGHTS

The Reliquary

Although not as extravagantly elaborate as the stunning Monasterio de las Descalzas, the Convento de la Encarnación is certainly worth a visit for its straightforward, laid back charm, and especially for its unique reliquary. Creeping around the deathly quiet and mysterious ancient buildings has quite a novel appeal, especially in a city as bustling as Madrid. Again, you're not going to be left in heavenly peace as you'll have to join one of the guided tours (usually in Spanish). Nuns of the Augustine Order still live in the convent.

The convent was established by Felipe III for his wife Margarita of Austria, who died shortly after work began, and was built to designs by Juan Gómez de Mora and Fray Alberto de la Madre de Dios in 1611. It has some decent paintings and sculptures from the 17th and 18th century, with works from Luca Giordano, Juan van der Hammen, Vicente Carducho, Gregorio Fernández and Pedro de Mena.

There's one work believed to be by José Ribera in the first room, while the second room is full of royal portraits. Fernández's grotesque *Recumbent Christ*, with its powerful contrast between light and shadow, and his *Flagellation* hang in the upper antichoir.

The atmospheric, almost library-like reliquary contains many hundreds of relics and artifacts from a long line of saints, though the guide is bound to focus on one, and for all good reason according to superstition. Apparently a great disaster is

Coin and stamp market on Plaza Mayor

impending if the blood of 4th-century saint Pantaleón, contained in a small glass phial, fails to liquefy at midnight every July 26—and it supposedly didn't liquefy during the Spanish Civil War. Rome, however, hasn't certified this one.

The impressive Latin-cross church was restored with marble in 1761 by Ventura Rodríguez, with Vicente Carducho topping off the altar with an *Annunciation*. Francisco Bayeu, Goya's influential brother-in-law, and the brothers González Velázquez, painted the ceiling frescoes that depict epic moments from the life of St Augustine.

Plaza Mayor

Once a no-nonsense market square that had it origins in the 15th century, the Plaza Mayor was transformed radically through Philip II's desire to create a square more worthy of the city's new status as imperial capital. Madrid took over from Toledo as capital of Spain in the mid-16th century. Some 20 years later, in 1561, Juan de Herrera was commissioned to create a grand central square, but his plans didn't get far past the drawing board. Juan Gómez de Mora inherited the task under Felipe III in 1617, and set to work to make up for lost time, finishing the job with impressive efficiency. Plaza Mayor as we see it now—at least more or less, for it has been subject to its fair share of fires and the like—was officially opened just two years later.

The building that most stands out is the two-towered Casa de la Panadería, which became the Baker's Guildhall and later—too good for bakers—a palace. It was begun by Diego Sillero in 1590 and ultimately became the fulcrum of Gómez de Mora's vision. Curiously, the square's oldest and most magnificent building's frescoes were added in only 1992. However, these funky modern creations of the allegories of Time, Climate, and Temperature by

Equestrian statue of Felipe III on Plaza Mayor

Carlos Franco somehow help to alleviate the museum-like appearance of the square, since Plaza Mayor is much more a monument and tourist attraction than a civic hub these days. A bronze equestrian statue of Felipe III, made by the great Flemish sculptor Giambologna in 1616, is situated in the middle of the square.

On Sundays Plaza Mayor plays host to a coin and stamp market and at Christmas is given over to countless stalls selling typical festive items and decorations. All in all it's a charming place to indulge in a drink or two, though do beware of the prices. It also has a welcoming and efficient tourist office.

Calle Postas, with decent bars and shops selling bizarre religious bric-à-brac, is an intriguing street. It makes a good route to Sol.

Puerta del Sol

While not the the centre of Madrid as it once was, Puerta del Sol is still very much a hub of central and older Madrid and even the centre of the country; a point through which visitors are bound to pass a number of times. It was once the eastern gate of old Madrid; the most prominent building today is the seat of the autonomous regional government, the Comunidad de Madrid, on the south side of the square. Built in 1766 by Jaime Marquet, it started life as a post office, Casa de Correos, during the reign of Carlos III. During the dark days of Franco it served a dubious role, housing the much-feared interior ministry and police headquarters. Prominent communist Julián Grimau was thrown from a window here in 1963. Now it evokes much more cheerful sentiment, especially as the locals pile into the square to hear Spain's best known clock chime the eight bells signalling the New Year as millions tune in on TV. Revellers try and stuff down 12 grapes (*uvas de la suerte*; grapes of good fortune), one for each month of the coming year, taken one at a time, in tandem with each chime of the clock and washed down by glasses of cava. The clock was added in 1866 and was designed by renegade clock maker Ramón Losada, who was forced to flee the country for his political beliefs.

Outside a slab of stone marks *kilómetro zero*: the exact point from which all distances in Spain are measured. Opposite, by the entrance of Calle del Carmen, stands a statue of a bear climbing a *madroño* (arbutus tree), a symbol of Madrid featured on its coat of arms.

Sol, perhaps unsurprisingly, has had a somewhat tumultuous history. On May 2 1808 it was the scene of slaughter, when Napoleon's troops entered Madrid at the outset of the Peninsular War and were met by stern local resistance. The event was later immortalised by Goya in his classic historical painting *Dos de Mayo*, which hangs in the Prado. No prizes for guessing who won, but suffice to say that Sol is where Wellington arrived in 1812 to lead an army of Spanish, English and Portuguese to victory over

Puerta del Sol

the French at Arapiles. Fernando VII was then ushered in as king here in 1814. To this day, there always seems to be a protest of some kind or other going on in Sol, and it is still a common meeting place, just as it was back in the 16th century.

in the area

Basilica de San Francisco El Grande *Plaza de San Francisco. Tours for a small fee.*
San Francisco El Grande has one of the largest domes in existence, 58 metres in height and 33 metres in diameter, painstakingly and stunning restored. As you enter the basilica, look out for a work by Goya, executed when the artist was in his mid-30s, in the first chapel on the left. The work depicts St Bernadino of Siena giving a sermon, but a self-portrait of the artist is also featured—on the right wearing yellow. There are also works by José de Ribera, Cano and Zurbarán, which can be seen if you join the guided tour.

Legend has it that a Franciscan monastery was founded on this spot by the one and only St Francis of Assisi in the early 13th century. When the original monastery was knocked down in 1760 during the reign of Carlos III, Ventura Rodríguez set to work on a new one, to plans inspired by St Peter's in Rome, though these were scotched in favour of those of rookie architect Brother Francisco Cabezas. The inexperienced Cabezas' plans proved to be unworkable once construction began, however, and Francesco Sabatini stepped in to save the day, completing the basilica in 1784. *M* La Latina **Map p. 68, C2**

Catedral de la Almudena *C/Bailén. Closed to visitors during mass.*
Madrid's cathedral is so new that it was actually consecrated by Pope John Paul II in 1993 and opened for worship in 1994, after much indecision and stalling.

Simply looking too new or too unoriginal to be a great or

The Catedral de la Almudena by night

spiritually uplifting cathedral (quite unlike Barcelona's mesmerising Sagrada Família), the lack of funds that plagued its construction and subsequent upkeep and are all too apparent. Despite having been started in the late 19th century, to this day it is still not completely finished. Different shades of light stonework create aesthetic disharmony, and this goes for both the exterior and the sparse neo-Gothic interior. Having said that, the creative ceiling murals carry a positive modern twist and make a welcome change from the Baroque cathedral standards to be found wherever the Counter Reformation once raged.

To the right of the main altar, in the Almudena Chapel, is a much more lavish altar that dates from the 16th century, with detailed canvases depicting biblical scenes. Also eye-catching are the *Arco Funerario de San Isidro* (the tapestry-decorated coffin of San Isidro directly behind the main altar) and the Capilla Opus Dei in honour of José María Escrivá de Balaguer, who founded the movement in Madrid.

The crypt, located at the back of the cathedral, is an altogether more mysterious affair, and it's quite eerie to wander around the scarcely lit individual chapels while anthems and motets such as *Ave Maria* break the deathly silence. The crypt is easy to miss as there's often nobody positioned on the door; just push the door on your right and let it close tight behind you.

A few metres further down Calle Mayor is the figure of the 'Virgen de la Almudena', and her past is the stuff of legend. When early Madrid was being invaded by the Moors, it is believed that the Christians hid her in the walls of a castle that once stood here. On re-conquering the city for the Spanish, Alfonso VI was desperate to find the Virgin again to reawaken Christian Madrid. A woman offered to sacrifice her life for the reappearance of the Virgin, and as the wall crumbled away to reveal her in all her resplendent beauty, the woman dropped to the ground and died instantly. *M* Ópera **Map p. 68, B2**

Ermita de la Virgen del Puerto The first building by legendary Madrid architect Pedro de Ribera—whose elaborate Baroque designs are credited with moving the city architecture on from the austere Habsburg period. This turreted, four-chapelled church is an important structure of Baroque Madrid. It was built in 1718 and was restored to its former glory after the Civil War in which it took a battering. *M* Príncipe Pío **Map p. 68, B1**

Iglesia de San Ginés *C/Arenal 13, T 91 366 4875. Free Admission.* One of Madrid's oldest churches, and one of the twelve parishes included in the 1202 charter. It was rebuilt in the mid 17th century by Juan Ruiz but experienced a number of fires; the most serious of which came in 1824 destroying some serious works of art. Today El Greco's *Expulsion from the Temple* plus works by Alonso Cano, Luca Giordano and Juan Martín Cabezalero can be found in the 17th-century Capilla del Cristo, the entrance to which is on Calle Bordadores. Famous parishioners include the 16th–17th-century playwright Lope de Vega and 17th-century poet Francisco de Quevedo, to whom there are plaques on the front façade. The atrium connecting to the street used to be a graveyard. *M* Sol **Map p. 68, B4**

San Isidro and his rescued son

Moorish Quarter and the Muralle Árabe (Arab Wall) Just to the south of Palacio Real, the Moorish quarter is one of the city's neighbourhoods and there's still a small length of 9th-century city wall standing, which was put up by the Moorish rulers. Popular for open-air theatre and concerts in the summer. *M* Ópera/La Latina **Map p. 68, C2**

Museo de San Isidro *Plaza de San Andrés 2, T 91 366 7415. Open Tues–Fri 9.30am–8pm and Sat–Sun 10am–2pm. Free Admission.* The archaeological collection charting the eras of human involvement in Madrid goes from Iron and Bronze Age artefacts found around the banks of the Manzanares, through the Visigoths and Moors up to the Habsburgs. There are also temporary exhibitions.

This is also the spot where Madrid's patron saint, San Isidro, a

12th-century agricultural labourer and well-digger, is said to have performed the most impressive of his miracles: rescuing his son from a well by raising the water level through prayer. The supposed well is still here, as well as a 17th-century chapel erected on the spot where San Isidro is believed to have died.

Isidro's miracles were sometimes performed in the spirit of the laid-back Madrileños of all eras: once he apparently fell asleep on the job, and two angels descended from heaven and put in a shift for him. He was beatified by Pope Paul V in 1618. *M* La Latina **Map p. 68, C3**

Plaza de Oriente Elegant square in front of the Royal Palace that came into being through Napoleon's big brother Joseph Bonaparte's desire to create the perfect view of the palace. Joseph Bonaparte was installed a King of Spain by Napoleon from 1808–13. The square is watched over by a statue of Felipe IV on horseback, and statues of other kings are also present in this most welcome pedestrian area. *M* Ópera **Map p. 68, B3**

Plaza de la Villa *Free guided tours in Spanish are available at 5pm and 6pm on Mondays.* Moorish and medieval Madrid's epicentre is the oldest surviving square in the city, and on it stands buildings of a melange of styles. The town hall (Ayuntamiento) or Casa de la Villa, on the west of the square, was designed by Juan Gómez de Mora and is a classic piece of Habsburg architecture. Tapestries adorn the grand staircase, while at the foot of the stairs the *Mariblanca* statue, which was originally placed on the fountain in the Puerta del Sol, looks on.

The Portrait Room has a number of royal portraits, none especially noteworthy. The official reception room is the Queen's Room, which opens onto the balcony and contains a painting of Christ by Francisco Rizzi as well as a copy of Goya's *Alegoría de la Villa de Madrid*, the original of which can be found in the Museo Municipal (*see p. 106*). The Assembly Room has late 17th-century ceiling frescoes by Antonio Palomino.

On the east side of the square is the Mudéjar-influenced Torre y Casa de Lujanes, which dates back to the 15th century, making it the oldest building on the Plaza and indeed amongst the oldest in all Madrid, though it was seriously restored in the 1920s. Just to add to the eclectic feel of the square the Mudéjar tower is topped off with a classically Gothic porch.

The statue in the centre of the square is Mariano Benlliure's depiction of Admiral Álvaro de Bazán, mastermind of the ill-fated Armada—the attempt by Spain to invade arch-rivals England.

The Casa de la Villa is connected to the plateresque Casa de Cisneros, built in 1537 by Benito Jiménez de Cisneros and restored in the early 20th century.

Calle del Codo, the narrowest street in Madrid, leads around the side of the tower to the tranquil Plaza del Conde de Miranda, and on the right stands the somewhat ordinary looking exterior of the Convento de las Carboneras, which belongs to the Spanish Hieronymite order. Inside however, the pint-sized church is quite a treat with sculptures from Antón de Morales and a painting of the *Last Supper* by Vicente Carducho. *M* Ópera **Map p. 68, B3**

River Manzanares Madrid's river is tucked away under a maze of flyovers heading into and out of town, though the Puente de Segovia is especially nice, perhaps too good for the stream that trickles beneath it. **Map p. 68, A1–D1**

Teatro Real *Plaza de Oriente, T 91 516 0606.* The Royal Theatre was built in the 19th century by López de Aguado and recently received a lavish €100 million modernisation, making it an even better venue for opera and ballet. *M* Ópera **Map p. 68, B3**

commercial galleries

Multiplicidad *C/Escalinata 1&15.* Worth a look for the wide variety of art forms on sale: paintings, sculptures, ceramics and various objects that make for gifts with a difference. The long list of painters represented includes Miren Aguirre, Ricardo Álvarez, Vicente Arnás, Marian Arzola, Badri, Manuel Barbero, Diego Balselga, Antonio Blanca, Enrico Bressan, Javier Lozano, Montse Roldos and Juan Romero. *M* Ópera **Map p.68, B3**

Galería Éboli *Plaza Ramales (corner of C/Santiago) T 91 547 1480*
www.galeriaeboli.com. Atmospherically housed in the old stables of the
palace of Count-Duke of Olivares, with no harm done to the original
architecture except for the welcome addition of a tiled floor, this
attractive exhibition space in the heart of the Madrid of the Asturias
hosts works from contemporary artists including Alfonso Galbis, Carmen
Gutiérrez Diaz and Rosa Susaeta. *M* Ópera **Map p. 68, B3**

eat

*Unless otherwise stated restaurants are open 1pm—4pm and 9pm—
midnight.*

RESTAURANTS

€€€ El Botín *C/Cuchilleros 17, T 91 366 4217.* One of Hemingway's
haunts, and the oldest restaurant in Europe (opened 1725)
according to the Guinness Book of Records. You might think this
would make the place a tourist nightmare. Miraculously, though, it
boasts a terrific atmosphere to this day, and the classic Castilian
roasts of suckling pig (*cochinillo*) and lamb (*cordero lechal*) are done
to perfection. You have a good chance of running into *la tuna*; not
the fish but the singing students dressed in the traditional garb. *M*
Tirso de Molina **Map p. 68, C3**

Casa Lucio *C/Cava Baja 35, T 91 365 3252.* A bastion of classic
Madrid cuisine popular with the rich and famous. Also serves the
most expensive egg and chips in town, though it sure is no ordinary
egg and chips. Reservations highly recommended. *M* La Latina **Map
p. 68, C3**

Posada de la Villa *C/Cava Baja 9, T 91 366 1860.* An age-old inn
dating back to 1642 and the days of the early Habsburgs.
Concentrates on hearty but refined classic Madrid cuisine.
Immensely popular for its lamb roasted in wood ovens as well as
cocido madrileño cooked slowly over the fire. *M* La Latina **Map p. 68,
C3**

El Botín

€€ **La Bola** *C/Bola 5, T 91 547 6930.* Attractive tiled restaurant still run by the family of its 19th-century founders. This place has claims to be the home of *cocido madrileño*, which is cooked temptingly in earthenware pots and is served at lunchtime only. *M* Ópera/Santo Domingo **Map p. 68, B3**

Café de Oriente *Plaza de Oriente 2, T 91 541 3974. Open 8.30 am–1.30am and 2.30am on Sat.* Elegant breakfast spot, similarly plush by night with lots of fine wine on offer. It's hard to beat the seats outside directly opposite the Palacio Real. Restaurant downstairs. *M* Ópera **Map p. 68, B3**

Casa Ciriaco *C/Mayor 84, T 91 548 0620.* Popular with Madrid's opinion-formers: artists and journalists, politicians and civil servants—even prime ministers and royalty. The thoroughly down-to-earth Ciriaco has been packing them in for years with its classic Madrid cuisine. Famous for *pepitoria de gallina* (chicken in an almond sauce). The partridge with beans is also well worth a go. Pictures of famous guests adorn the walls. *M* Ópera **Map p. 68, B4**

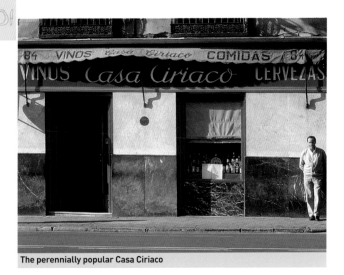

The perennially popular Casa Ciriaco

Juanalaloca *Plaza Puerta de Moros 4, T 91 364 0525.* International and Spanish cuisine with a strong Basque influence from Isabel Tocchetti and Pancho Bonasso, who serve up dishes such as pickled caramelised foie with couscous and a new take on the Spanish omelette. Daily menu costs €12, served weekdays. *M* La Latina **Map p. 68, C3**

BARS & TAPAS

El Anciano Rey de los Vinos *C/Bailén 19, T 91 559 5332.* Dating back to 1909, long before the cathedral that lies directly opposite was much more than a sparkle in the town planners' eye, this bar serves a good range of traditional tapas and has a decent selection of reds from Rioja, Ribera del Duero and Valdepeñas, as well as whites and rosés available by the glass. **Map p. 68, B3**

As de los Vinos *C/Paz 4.* Feisty Valdepeñas wines, dry or sweet, in classic old tiled bar famous for its *torrijas*: deep-fried dough dipped in wine and covered in sugar and spice. There are also other good value tapas, such as *bonito en escabeche* (marinated tuna). A sister bar to the El Anciano above. *M* Sol **Map p. 68, B4**

Los Caracoles *Plaza de Cascorro 18, T 91 527 7707.* A fine place to try snails cooked in a thick spicy sauce, the speciality of the house, or other tapas washed down by ice-cold beer or *vermut* that can be a welcome treat after negotiating the nearby Rastro. *M* La Latina **Map p. 68, C4**

Casa Labra *C/Tetuán 12, T 91 531 0081.* Popular and traditional tapas joint dating back to 1869, serving up freshly cooked *bacalao* (salted cod) either fried in batter or in croquettes. The restaurant at the back serves local classics. The Spanish Socialist Party (PSOE) was founded here in 1879. Fine old décor. *M* Sol **Map p. 68, B4**

Larios Café *C/Silva 4, T 91 547 9394. Open 8pm–5am every day.* Much more than a café, très chic Larios is also a cocktail lounge and hosts regular live music. There's dancing downstairs and Cuban food served upstairs. *M* Santo Domingo/Callao **Map p. 68, B4**

La Taberna de Antonio Sánchez *C/Mesón de Paredes 13, T 91 539 7826.* Dating back to 1830, this wonderful traditional Madrid bar was taken over by the first Antonio Sánchez in the late 19th century, and was later run by his son of the same name when he hung up his bullfighting cape. Hence the bulls' heads staring down at the zinc-topped bar. His paintings also adorn the dark walls.

Tapas-wise, it's known for its *montados*: various tangy toppings spread on crusty bread. *M* Tirso de Molina **Map p. 68, C4**

Taberna de los Cien Vinos *C/Nuncio 17, T 91 365 4704.* In the converted stables of the adjoining Palacio de Anglona, off Plaza de la Paja. Sophisticated tapas and wines, a lot of which are available by the glass, in a reassuringly down-to-earth setting. Lots of daily specials available. Look out for *pastel de puerros*, a leek tart. *M* La Latina **Map p. 68, C3**

Taberna Tempranillo *C/Cava Baja 38, T 91 364 1532.* Top place for a glass of fine wine, be it from the Tempranillo grape or just about anything else from Spain. A Flamenco soundtrack accompanies the wine and the quality tapas. *M* La Latina **Map p. 68, C3**

CAFÉS

Anticafé *C/Unión 2, T 91 559 4163.* Quirky arty hangout in a labyrinth setting with jam sessions, DJs and projection shows. Serves food to go with the ambience. *M* Ópera **Map p. 68, B3**

Café del Monaguillo *Plaza de la Cruz Verde 3, T 91 541 2941.* Good range of coffees with a pleasant interior. Its gorgeous terrace on the Plaza is a must when the weather permits, which in Madrid is a fair chunk of the time. *M* La Latina **Map p. 68, C3**

Chocolatería de San Ginés *Pasadizo de San Ginés 5, T 91 365 6546.* A Madrid institution, and just the place to get some sticky dough covered in chocolate—*churros con chocolate*—down after a night on the tiles. Opens in the evening and pushes through past dawn, catering for revellers pouring out of nearby nightspots. *M* Sol **Map p. 68, B4**

Delic *C/Costanilla de San Andrés 14, T 91 364 5450.* Café/cocktail bar-cum-delicatessen serving savoury crêpes, salads, banana, chocolate, apple and carrot cakes, and classic Latin American cocktails like mojitos, caipiriñas and piña colada. Terrace looks out onto Plaza de la Paja. *M* La Latina **Map p. 68, C3**

shop

Shopping in this part of town veers on the touristy, especially around the visitor magnet of Plaza Mayor, though there are still some excellent shops to be found. Madrid's antiques scene is centred down in La Latina, which every Sunday witnesses the huge extravaganza of the Rastro market, which ranges from serious antiquities, a plethora of relatively useful bric-à-brac to complete and utter junk. All the same, it's a defining Madrid experience to wander around it and then be swept away in the post-Rastro atmosphere in the close-at-hand bars and fine eateries around Calle de la Cava, Calle Cuchilleros and Plaza de la Cebada.

Note that many shops in Madrid, particularly the old-fashioned kind, take a siesta break until 5pm.

ACCESSORIES

Casa de Diego *Puerta del Sol 12.* Superb old-style accessories that are still in demand—from the likes of the British Royal family, no less. Has been selling fans, umbrellas, shawls and dapper walking sticks since 1853. Also does repairs. *M* Sol **Map p. 68, B4**

Casa Jiménez *C/Preciados 42.* The idea of Spanish damsels wafting fans all day may be as outdated as them clicking castanets at every opportunity, though that said there's room for a certain amount of sentiment for the exquisite fans on offer here. The same goes for the shawls. *M* Callao **Map p. 68, B4**

ANTIQUES

Rastro *C/Ribera de Curtidores.* Boasting over 1,000 stalls and dating back to the 15th century, the sprawling chaos of the Rastro flea markets certainly merits a saunter around, even if you're not looking for anything.

From early morning to 3pm on Sundays, though more and more on Fridays, Saturdays and holidays, crowds flock to the market that flows and ebbs along C/Ribera de Curtidores from the Plaza de Cascorro to the Ronda de Toledo. Everything under the sun can be found here, from antiques of varying quality to used clothing, including collector cards, books, records, paintings, freshly stolen tourist goodies, kitchen sinks,

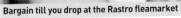

Bargain till you drop at the Rastro fleamarket

etc. For many it's simply a place to hang out. For higher-end antiques head to the permanent shops nearby, though you never know—you might just strike gold rummaging around the stalls. The local restos and bars get packed as the market winds down and the gaggle turns its attention to a drink and a good feed.

Watch out for pickpockets and bag-snatchers here. And don't make the mistake of arriving by car: parking is impossible. *M* La Latina/Puerta de Toledo **Map p. 68, C4–D4**

Galerías Piquer *C/Ribera de Curtidores 29. Open 10.30 am–2pm every day, plus 5pm–8pm Mon–Fri.* More than 70 shops are grouped together under one roof in this one-stop antiques arcade. A host of antiques, and paintings from the likes of Sorolla. *M* Puerta de Toledo **Map p. 68, D4**

Antigüedades de Oficina *C/Arganzuela 29.* One for the olde worlde office hardware fanatic, selling inkwells, desks, typewriters, all manner of calculating machines, pencil sharpeners, paperweights, all at least half a century old. *M* Puerta de Toledo **Map p. 68, D3**

El Transformista *C/Mira el Río Baja.* Now we're well into the 21st century: items from the 1950s and 1960s could well be considered antiques. *M* Puerta de Toledo **Map p.68, D3**

CLOTHES

Fetish by Fabio Alexandrino *Costanilla de los Ángeles 7.* Racy but elegant evening wear made out of latex, acrylic, aluminium and all kinds of other materials. More sophisticated than it sounds. *M* Ópera/Santa Domingo **Map p. 68, B3**

Casa Yustas *Plaza Mayor 30. Open Mon–Sat 9.30am–9.30pm and 11am–1.30pm Sun.* The oldest hat shop in Madrid, dating back to 1894 and just the place to come for a classic Spanish titfer, whether it be a *sombrero*, or one of those *bionas* (berets) that quite a few of the locals wear. Good place for gifts. Doesn't take credit cards, never has done, never will. *M* Sol **Map p. 68, B4**

One-Way *C/Santiago 1.* Casual and smart casual menswear with smart, suitably restrained designs. Exclusive distributor of BZR and Bruuns Bazaar in Spain. *M* Ópera **Map p.68, B3**

Zara *C/Preciados.* Remarkable prices, quite a lot cheaper than you'll find outside Spain for smart everyday wear as well as pretty convincing copies/reproductions of what's big on the catwalk a short time before. The mass-market take on couture lines has taken off big-time, both nationally and internationally. There are branches of this Galician-founded fashion house all over the city, though this one caters for women, men and children—and gets packed out with bargain-hunters on Saturdays. *M* Sol **Map p. 68, B4**

CRAFTS

Antigua Casa Talavera *C/Isabel la Católica 2*. Top ceramics shop specialising in Valencian tiles, plus the blue and yellow Talavera type, too. Replicas of Spanish (and indeed Moorish-influenced) tiles from the 10th to the 18th centuries. The shop itself is of course beautifully decorated with its wares. *M* Santo Domingo **Map p. 68, B3**

El Arco de los Cuchilleros *Plaza Mayor 9*. Unexpected and varied Spanish craft items made from leather, ceramic and wood, sourced from all over the country courtesy of the store's close relationship with many workshops and artisans. *M* Sol/Ópera **Map p. 68, B4**

Rústika Alfonso *C/Alfonso VI*. Creative decorations and gift items made from all kinds of materials and colours using crystal, chrome from tin, resins, and embroidered fabrics. *M* La Latina/Ópera **Map p. 68, C3**

DEPARTMENT STORES

El Corte Inglés *C/Preciados 1, 2 & 3; Plaza de Callao 2*. It's quite hard to imagine Spanish cities without El Corte. Everything you need under one roof—well not quite. This branch is so huge that they've had to take up several premises on the same street. Music, videos, computers and other electronic goods at 1, books at number 2, all manner of clothing including big-name labels and supermarket at 3—and that's just the tip of the iceberg. Wherever you go you will keep on running into branches of El Corte Inglés. *M* Sol/Callao **Map p. 68, B4**

FOOD

Come Bio *C/Mayor 30*. Healthy-looking organic produce in a shop that seeks to educate a not particularly bio-minded public. Restaurant attached serving good value set menus, with organic alcoholic beverages enabling partakers to get ever so healthily drunk. *M* Sol **Map p. 68, B4**

La Exquisita *Plaza Puerta de Moros 2*. Cute delicatessen stacked with enticing goodies, both Spanish and foreign, owned and run by the friendly Inma, a wine enthusiast who also holds tastings in the shop. There's also a tasting area where you can try what's on show, washed down with a glass of wine at better prices than in many of the nearby posh tapas joints. *M* La Latina **Map p. 68, C3**

The classic Spanish accessory

La Mallorquina *Puerta del Sol 2.* Timeless classic of a pastry shop with goodies galore to tickle your fancy. All smells great too. Café upstairs looking out onto Sol. *M* Sol **Map p. 68, B4**

Mercado de la Cebada *Plaza de la Cebada.* Colourful neighbourhood market where literally each and every humanly edible part of a dead animal can be bought, along with ripe, fresh fruit and veg, and a very good selection of fish and cheese. *M* La Latina **Map p. 68, C3**

Mercado de San Miguel *Open Mon–Sat 9am–2pm & 5pm–8pm.* Close to the Plaza Mayor, this restored 19th-century indoor market is a good place to stock up on fresh foodstuffs. *M* Sol **Map p. 68, B3**

La Oriental *C/Campomanes 5.* Haven for chocolate and coffee lovers. Traditionally-made goodies, with a focus on Central European delicacies. *M* Ópera **Map p. 68, B3**

El Palacio de los Quesos *C/Mayor 53.* A great place to get acquainted with the vast and varied Spanish cheese scene. There's much more than the ubiquitous *manchego* on offer at the 'Palace of Cheeses', with 80 types of cheese from all around the country. *M* Sol/Ópera **Map p. 68, B4**

JEWELLERY

Carmen Pasión *C/Mesonero Romanos 3*. A wide choice of designer silver and imitation jewellery for both sexes, plus textiles and other gifts. Watches from Breil, D&G and Guess, though there are some really cheap watches to be found as well, starting at 11.95! *M* Sol/Callao **Map p. 68, B4**

02 *C/Carmen 8*. Silver, imitation designer and costume jewellery plus many styles of watches downstairs, with textile accessories, gifts and décor items upstairs. *M* Sol **Map p. 68, B4**

MUSIC

El Flamenco Vive *C/Conde de Lemos 7*. Claims the most comprehensive Flamenco collection on the planet. Also sells handmade guitars, castanets, Flamenco outfits, as well as books, videos, photos and sheet music. *M* Ópera **Map p. 68, B3**

José Ramírez *C/Concepción Jerónima*. Legendary guitar makers that also houses a museum of antique instruments. *M* Tirso de Molina **Map p. 68, C4**

SPECIALIST

Iberdanza Madrid *C/Felipe V 2*. Devoted solely to ballet, María Corella and husband Mariano set up this exquisite shop with leotards galore to fill a market niche, becoming the first shop in Madrid to cater exclusively to ballet dancers. Its hottest items are its Gaynor Minden pointe shoes. *M* Ópera **Map p. 68, B3**

Palomeque *C/Arenal 17*. Fascinating museum-like shop stacked with religious articles that's interesting for a browse, even for dogged agnostics. One of Palomeque's specialities is its crucifixes. The business has been around since 1873, so there must be some fervent believers out there in the mêlée somewhere. *M* Sol/Ópera **Map p. 68, B4**

WINE & SPIRITS

Mariano Madrueño *C/Postigo San Martín 3*. Grand selection of Spanish wines from a charming old distributor who has been in business since 1895. Also some interesting liquors and spirits such as the Navarran Pacharán, beefed up and infused with sloes. *M* Callao **Map p. 68, B4**

CHUECA & MALASAÑA

CHUECA & MALASAÑA

1 0 300 yards
0 300 metres

2　**3**　**4**

A

Pl. del Cardinal Cisneros

Arco de la Victoria

C. del Obispo

Trav. de A. Nebrija

Avenida

VALLEHERMOSO

Paseo de San Francisco de Sales

C. de Doménico Scarlatti

Isaac Peral

Aviación Esp.

Islas Filipinas

Calle

Estava

Gaztambide

Guzmán

Andrés

Joaquín

María

Museo de América

Faro de Madrid

Reyes Católicos

Min. Ibáñez Martín

Arco de la Victoria

Calle

Hilarión

B

Parque

Chapi

Moret

Monctoa

Ruperto

GAZTAMBIDE

Fernández

Fernando

Basco

F. Garri

del

Paseo

Paseo Lisboa

Ecija

Fr. de S. Juan Bosco

Lozano

Romero

Robledo

Gutiérrez

Benito

Altamirano

Meléndez

Palomino

Rodríguez

F. de Ricci

E. Carr

Oeste

ARGÜELLES

Camoens

F. y J. Alcantara

Calle

Ferraz

Paseo

Calle

del Marqués

de Urquijo

Martín

Argüelles

Serrano Joyer

Santa

Albert

C

Estación del Teleférico Casa del Campo

Plaza Argüelles

Buen Suceso

Quintana

Francisco Seminario de Nobles

Centro Cultural Conde Duque Museo de Arte Contemporáneo

Juan

del

Rey

Ventura Rodríguez

Ermita de San Antonio de la Florida

Av. de Valladolid

Ribera

Pte. de Reina Victoria

Pintor Rosales

Ev. Miguel

C. de Álvarez

Luisa Fernanda

Tutor

Fernando

Plaza del Marqués de Carralbo

Plaza del Marqués de Carralbo

Mediarralbo

Ventura Rodríguez S.M.

Marcela

Heros

Museo Cerralbo

Plaza de España

D

Paseo

de

Rosales

Aniceto

de Río Manzanares

Templo de Debod

Calle de Ferraz

Plaza de España

San Vicente

Marqués de Monistrol

Mozart

Florida

Marthas

E. Rey

Benot

C. de Illustración

Estación de Príncipe Pío

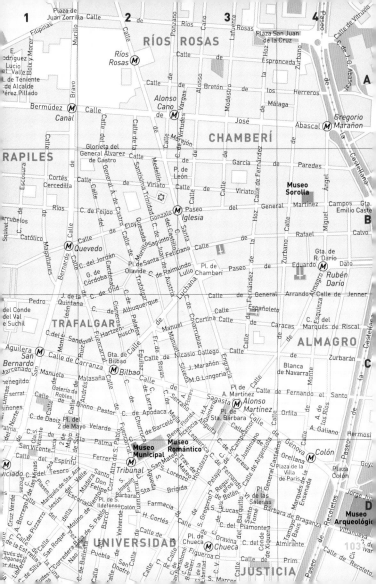

Just a few steps away from the bustling Gran Vía the atmosphere changes from big city to reassuringly local and intimate. The two districts of Malasaña and Chueca are noticeably distinct from one another, and both warrant plenty of time wandering around. In fact both areas are best navigated on foot, and quite simply the more you're prepared to wander the more you'll find. This part of town is densely packed with art treasures and a fair bite of the city's tantalising nightlife. Chueca in particular has scores of galleries, though you'll find a few in deeper Malasaña too. Chueca can be somewhat dodgy in one or two places, though you're unlikely just to wander in there unawares.

Museo Municipal

OPEN	Tues–Fri 9.30am–8pm, Sat–Sun 10am–2pm.
CLOSED	Mondays and holidays
CHARGES	Admission free
TELEPHONE	91 588 8672
WEB	www.munimadrid.es
MAIN ENTRANCE	C/Fuencarral 78
DISABLED ACCESS	No
METRO	Tribunal
SERVICES	Shop

HIGHLIGHTS

Baroque entrance designed by Pedro de Ribera

Alegoría de la Villa de Madrid (1810) – **Goya**

Wooden scale model of 1830 Madrid – **Leon Gil de Palacio**

The Municipal Museum is in the second phase of it rehab, and renovations are unlikely to be complete until 2007 at the earliest, though most of the museum's highlights are on view in the limited exhibition space. In fact the real highlight is on the outside of this former hospice, orphanage and poorhouse built by de Ribera in the early 18th century: the striking and elaborate Baroque entrance, designed by Pedro de Ribera and sculpted by Juan Ron. On the inside, the superbly crafted model of Madrid by Colonel Leon Gil de Palacio depicts the layout of Madrid as it was in 1830, before it sprawled off into the distance. The 5.2 by 3.5-metre

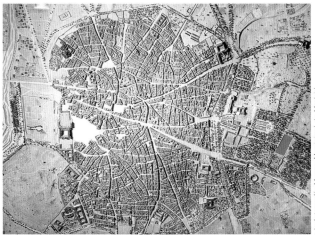

Wooden model of 19th-century Madrid

© de la fotografía Museo Municipal de Madrid

Goya: *Alegoría de la Villa de Madrid* (1810)

© de la fotografía Museo Municipal de Madrid

wooden scale model of the city took the colonel two years of painstaking work and was completed in 1830 at the end of the reign of Fernando VII, just before the introduction of a new law led to the ripping down of many convents and monasteries.

Of the paintings Goya's *Alegoría de la Villa de Madrid* (1810) is the biggest draw. The allegorical painting is a celebration of an uprising against the occupying French that occurred on May 2nd 1808, and features heavenly figures holding aloft a plaque with the symbolic date on it. There are also a couple of works by one of Goya's pupils, José del Castillo. While his paintings are Goyaesque and are of some stature, the master proved a hard act to follow.

Jenaro Pérez Villamil's *Vista del Palacio de Madrid* (1854) is a good example of 19th-century Spanish Realism. Juan de la Corte's *Fiesta in the Plaza Mayor* is interesting from a historical perspective. When fully operational there will be further objects, paintings and models on display from the Habsburg and Bourbon periods. While hardly enticingly named, and often neglected, the Museo Municipal provides a fascinating insight into the city's development, and its collection has always been somewhat eclectic, just like the city itself. The museum also has two mini Sorollas from the Valencian artist's early phase. There are comfy seats outside from where you can sit and admire de Ribera's splendid entrance.

Museo Cerralbo

OPEN	Tues–Sat 9.30am–3pm, Sun and public holidays 10am–3pm
CLOSED	Mondays, 1/1, 1/5, 24/12, 25/12 31/12
CHARGES	€2.40. Under 18, over 65 and retired free
TELEPHONE	91 547 36 46
WEB	www.museocerralbo.mcu.es
MAIN ENTRANCE	C/Ventura Rodriguez 17
DISABLED ACCESS	Yes
METRO	Ventura Rodríguez/Plaza de España

HIGHLIGHTS

Ecstasy of St Francis **by El Greco**

Lavish ballroom

Left exactly as the 17th Marquis of Cerralbo, Enrique Aguilera y Gamboa, decreed upon his death in 1922, this museum is a fantastic jumble of his former art treasures and a veritable trip back in time.

Cerralbo was an influential politician, a pioneering archaeologist, and passionate art collector. With no heir to inherit his magnificent collection, he left his home and its contents to the state with the intention that it be converted into a museum.

The rich collection covers European art from the 16th–19th centuries: sculptures, drawings, prints, coins, medals, various archaeological finds, arms and armour. There's also a host of decorative arts spanning different periods and styles with ceramics, clocks, lamps, jewels, carpets and tapestries. Despite the obvious luxury of the place, the amiable clutter and the sheer amount of stuff give the museum a most homely feel.

On the ground floor the Religious Gallery to the left of the 'great staircase' leads to the Chapel. As soon as you set foot inside this place of family worship, you are greeted by El Greco's dark and brooding *Ecstasy of St Francis*, depicting the saint receiving the stigmata.

Paintings by Alonso Cano, Bartolomé González, Francisco de Zurbarán, José de Ribera and Paul de Vos are usually hung in the Picture Gallery, but are sometimes moved around if there's a temporary exhibition on, so it can pay to ask the Cerralbo's helpful staff where things are.

The Music Room has portraits of Felipe V and Maria Luisa Gabriela of Savoy by Miguel Jacinto Meléndez from around 1712, while the Family Dining Room has still life paintings by Juan de Arellano, Margherita Caffi and Giovanni Battista Ruoppolo.

Things get more luxurious upstairs, in apartments that the marquis opened up just once a week to entertain guests at parties and balls. The galleries are plushly decorated with crystal chandeliers from La Granja and Venice and 18th- and 19th-century porcelain and furniture. In the Billiard Room is a billiard table which once belonged to Fernando VII. Note the rather long cue. Quite apart from the fact that it looks more like a weapon, the multi-faceted marquis must have been pretty deft to pot any balls with it.

The outlandish Ballroom with its surround mirrors is out of this world, and even acts as a reminder of our mortality—the marquis had to leave all this glittering splendour behind. There's a portrait of the man himself hanging in Gallery 1, next to the Ballroom.

Museo Municipal de Arte Contemporáneo

OPEN	Tues–Sat 10am–2pm and 5.30pm–9pm, Sun and holidays 10.30am–2.30pm
CLOSED	Mondays
CHARGES	Free
TELEPHONE	91 588 59 28

WEB	www.munimadrid.es/museoartecontemporaneo/
ENTRANCE	C/Conde Duque 9 and 11, located in the Centro Cultural del Conde Duque
METRO	San Bernardo/Argüelles/Plaza de España

HIGHLIGHTS

Eduardo Arroyo – *Madrid-Paris-Madrid*

Esteban Vicente – *Environment*

Luis Gordillo – *Potemkin*

Fernando Bellver – *Grabado de Madrid*

Opened in 2001, the Museum of Contemporary Art is the new kid on the art museum block and is a nicely laid out and positive addition to the Madrid art scene. If you like modern art, this is definitely the place for you. The permanent collection is housed on the first and second floors.

FIRST FLOOR

This is given over to works acquired by the museum between 1999 and 2001, representing the plethora of contemporary artistic styles that took root in Madrid soil. Artists exhibited include Joaquín Torres García, Rafael Canogar, Alfaro, Antonio Saura, Francisco Ferreras, Susana Solano, Ouka Lele, David Lechuga, Laura Lío, Pelayo Ortega, Ralph Fleck and José Luis Pastor.

SECOND FLOOR

Here the exhibit is arranged chronologically and artists are subdivided into schools or by artistic tendencies. The collection begins with the School of Madrid and 'Las Vanguardias Históricas', with works by Francisco Borres, Daniel Vázquez Díaz, Benjamín Palencia, José Caballero, Álvaro Delgado and Agustín Redondela.

The continuation pays homage to the 'Masters of Abstraction'— the initiators of the movement in Spain—with paintings by Lucio

Muñoz, Manuel Rivera, Gustavo Torner and Fernando Zóbel. The new figurative and abstract art of the 1980s is represented by Luis Gordillo, Eduardo Arroyo, Manolo Valdés, Eduardo Úrculo, Alfonso Fraile, Carlos Franco and the abstractionists Juan Navarro Baldeweg, Alfonso Albacete, Marta Cárdenas and Miguel Ángel Campano among others. Realists are represented by intimate, urban, and dramatic styles from artists including Amalia Avia, Isabel Quintanilla, Daniel Quintero, Jose Manuel Ballester, Juan Moreno Aguado, Félix de la Concha, Luis Mayo, Carlos Díez Bustos and Chiti Ayuso.

The final section of 'Nuevos Creadores' is a mixed bag of current styles of both figurative and abstract art, including Javier de Juan, Juan Ugalde, Juan Carlos Savater, Abraham Lacalle, Alejandro Corujeira, Alberto Reguera, Javier Riera and Xavier Grau.

Ermita de San Antonio de la Florida

OPEN	Tues–Fri 10am–2pm and 4pm–8pm
CHARGES	Free entrance
TELEPHONE	91 542 0722
WEB	www.munimadrid.es
ENTRANCE	Glorieta de San Antonio de la Florida 5
METRO	Príncipe Pío

HIGHLIGHTS

Goya's tomb

Frescoes by Goya

Goya's final resting place is a must for the incredible frescoes painted by the master, which helped propel him to prominence and which are now located almost directly above his tomb.

This small Neoclassical church, constructed on a Greek cross plan, was built on the request of Carlos IV by the Italian Filippo Fontana, between 1792 and 1798. Goya's job was to decorate it— and decorate it he did, with some of his most powerful use of light and character depiction.

Looking up, celestial angels and cherubs draw back curtains to reveal a miracle being performed in the nick of time by San Antonio de la Florida, to save his father who was falsely accused of murder. Goya pictures the saint at the point of resurrecting the murdered man, who declares that it was not his father who carried out the foul deed.

The jury is out on whether the onlookers were modelled on peasants or in fact on the Madrid movers and shakers of the day; whichever it was, they are remarkably realistic. What is certain is that Goya took prostitutes as his models for the 'fallen' angels who adorn the apse (*pictured overleaf*). The 'fallen' angels have themselves have been brought painstakingly back to life after years of restoration work, and possess a certain sadness that goes beyond words and well beyond the celestial world.

Goya's remains were transferred to the Ermita in 1919 from where he was first laid to rest in Bordeaux, though apparently minus his head.

Next door is an identical church that is used for worship, so that the Ermita can be devoted to Goya's frescoes.

Goya's 'fallen angels' in the Ermita de San Antonio de la Florida (1798)

Museo de América

OPEN	Tues–Sat 10am–3pm, Sundays and holidays 10am–2.30pm
CLOSED	Mondays
CHARGES	€3.00; €1.5 reduced admission, free on Sundays and holidays. Free admission ticket for over 65s and under 18s.
TELEPHONE	91 549 2641 and 91 543 9437
WEB	www.museodeamerica.mcu.es
MAIN ENTRANCE	Avenida de los Reyes Católicos 6
METRO	Moncloa

Just the place to check out what Spain appropriated, other than gold, during its time as the lord of much of Latin America. Complementing the city's concentration on Spanish and European art, the Museo de América draws on some rich cultural pickings from Spain's colonial past, covering the Aztec, Maya and Inca cultures in depth.

Of special interest is the famous Cortesano Manuscript—the Tro-Cortesian Codex (also known as the Madrid Codex)—one of four remaining Mayan manuscripts. Its 56 pages contain hieroglyphics and scenes from everyday life, captured probably in the century before the arrival of the Spanish. It contains particular dates, based on the 260-day Tzolkin calendar, that have religious and supernatural meaning. See also the Tudela Codex, which portrays the fateful arrival of the Spanish.

This collection of pre-Columbian art and anthropological items from all parts of the one-time Spanish Americas is a must for anyone interested in native American culture or in non-European art forms. It's sadly apparent how these indigenous cultures came to a grinding halt after the arrival of the Spanish *conquistadores*.

in the area

Plaza de España The Franco era's architectural stamp on Madrid can perhaps best be felt in this square, through two colossal, and some would say bombastic, buildings. At the top of the square the brick and limestone Edificio España, designed by Joaquín and Julián Otamendi, was the highest of them all when it went up in 1953. The 26 level building was originally planned to be a self-contained, fully functioning, state-of-the-art 'enclosed village', with all needs catered for under one roof. The brothers then added the adjacent 32-storey Torre de Madrid in 1957.

The statues of Cervantes's immortal Don Quixote and his ever-faithful sidekick Sancho Panza were sculpted by Coullaut Valera, to designs by Teodoro Anasagasti and Mateo Inurria. *M* Plaza de España **Map p. 102, D3–D4**

Templo de Debod *Open Apr–Sep Tue–Fri 10am–2pm and 6pm–8pm, Sat–Sun 10am–2pm; Oct–Mar Tue–Fri 9.45am–1.45pm and 4pm–6pm, Sat–Sun 10am–2pm. Closed Mon and holidays.* Madrid's oldest building by far, although an import—a gift from the Egyptian state in return for Spain's help in rescuing ancient relics during the construction of a dam. The ancient Egyptian temple dates back to the 4th century BC, though it came to the Spanish capital only in 1970. It now occupies the spot where revolting Madrileños were shot by the occupying French on May 3, 1808. *M* Ventura Rodríguez **Map p. 102, D3**

Faro de Madrid *Avda de los Reyes Católicos. T 91 544 8104. Small entrance fee.* Superb viewpoint from 92 metres up, with stunning views across the city and out to the Sierra de Guadarrama mountain range. This futuristic structure, designed by Salvador Pérez Arroyo, was constructed in 1992 to coincide with Madrid's role as the European Capital of Culture, and also the 500th anniversary of Spain's discovery of America. It is in fact located just in front of the Museo de América. Pleasantly uncrowded and off the heavily beaten tourist track—but don't expect a bar at the top. *M* Moncloa **Map p. 102, A2**

Museo Romántico *C/San Mateo 13, T 91 445 6402. Closed at the time of writing with no date given for its reopening.* When open, the Museo Romántico takes visitors back to the Romantic era of the 19th century, a period and an attitude to life and art which stretched from the 1820s and reached its zenith in the reign of Queen Isabel II (1833–68). Its exhibit focuses on the art, furnishings, decorative objects and documents from that time. Before closing for renovation it housed Goya's *San Gregorio*, which was located in the chapel. *M* Tribunal **Map p. 103, D2**

Sociedad General de Autores y Editores *C/Fernando VI 4, T 91 349 9622.* This seemingly Gaudíesque building, that could be said to resemble a wobbly, custard-coloured wedding cake, and which is now home to the society of writers and publishers, was built in 1902 by José Grases Riera as the headquarters of the Longoria Bank. Riera is thought to have been more influenced by Hector Guimard, who designed the original Paris Metro entrances, than the Catalan *modernistas*. Even so, it still has a faint air of Barcelona about it. It's generally not open to the public, though there's no harm in poking your head around the entrance to sneak a peek at the courtyard. *M* Chueca/Alonso Martínez **Map p. 103, D3**

commercial galleries

Alcion Art Gallery *C/Orellana 14 (on the corner of Argensola), T 91 319 3037.* Quality reproductions of a wide gamut of classic and more modern paintings by Spanish and foreign artists. Prices start at €300 and go up to a couple of thousand. *M* Alonso Martínez/Colón **Map p. 103, D3**

Antonio Machón *C/Conde de Xiquena 8, T 91 532 4093.* Since 1973 Machón has been dealing with some of the cream of established Spanish artists as well as many of the up-and-coming generation. Works from Barjola, Bonifacio, Chema Cobo, Chillida, Delgado, Garmendia, Giralt, Gordillo, José Guerrero, Xavier Grau, Guinovart, Lazkano, María Gómez, Oteiza,

Reguera, Rojas, San José, Saura, Savater, Tàpies, Teixidor and Vigil. **M** Chueca **Map p. 103, D3**

Bat Alberto Cortejo C/Ríos Rosas 54, T 91 554 4810. Dealing principally with contemporary art, Bat focuses on graphic art, as well as figurative and abstract paintings and sculpture from both Spanish and foreign artists. Features work from the likes of Picasso, Tàpies, Chillida and the El Paso group (see Reina Sofía), to Concha Hermosilla, Miguel Peña, David Lechuga, José Luis Alesanco, Paco Lagares, Montse Casacuberta, Titi Pedroche and Luis Feito. Its shop also sells objets d'art. **M** Ríos Rosas **Map p. 103, A3**

Edurne C/Justiniano 3, T 91 310 0651 www.galeriaedurne.com. In its 40 years of existence paintings by contemporary icons Antoni Tàpies and Antonio Saura have hung on its walls. More recently Ernesto Knorr, Andrés Monteagudo, Marcela Navascués and Enrique Veganzones have exhibited in this gallery, run by Margarita de Lucas and Antonio de Navascués. **M** Alonso Martínez **Map p. 103, D3**

Elba Benítez C/San Lorenzo 11, T 91 310 0651 www.elbabenitez.com. Cutting-edge works in attractive setting from Spanish and non-Spanish artists, focusing largely on photography, video and installation. Committed to promoting both locals and foreigners on the international stage such as Ignasi Aballi, Miriam Bäckström, Juan Cruz, El Último Grito, Fernanda Fragateiro, Carlos Garaicoa, José Antonio Hernández-Díez, Cristina Iglesias, Juan Luis Moraza, Vik Muniz, Ernesto Neto, Francisco Ruiz de Infante, Francesc Torres, Valentín Vallhonrat and Joana Vasconcelos. **M** Tribunal **Map p. 103, D2**

Estampa C/Justiniano 6, T 91 308 3030, www.galeriaestampa.com. Since its foundation in 1978, Estampa's goal had been the spreading of contemporary Spanish and foreign artists of the 'Nueva Figuración', a movement which has its roots in the art of Francis Bacon, the COBRA group and Willem de Kooning, representing reality as a naked truth, with all the monstrosity and grotesqueness that that sometimes entails. Artists represented include Fernando Álamo, Jaime Aledo, Isabel Baquedano, Cuasante, Ramiro Fernández Saus, Carlos Forns Bada, Emilio González Sáinz, Jorge García Pfretzschner, Sara Huete, Ramón Losa, Luis Mayo, José Luis Mazario, Joaquín Millán, Juan Moreno Aguado, Inmaculada Salinas and Concha Ybarra. Estampa also publishes limited-edition books, including La Biblioteca de Alejandría, El traje de tus versos or Poetas y Pintores. In these collections, Estampa's artists work with contemporary poets. **M** Alonso Martínez **Map p. 103, D2**

Estiarte C/Almagro 44, T 91 308 15 69. A stronghold of Spanish graphic art for three decades, including Picasso, Chillida, Miró, Rueda, Broto,

Barceló, Jaume Plensa and José María Sicilia. Also deals with a few international artists. *M* Rubén Darío **Map p. 103, C4**

Fúcares *C/Conde de Xiquena 12, T 91 308 0191*. Owner Norberto Dotor has a reputation for championing young artists. Artists represented here include Ángel Bados, Elena Blasco, Isidro Blasco, Patricio Cabrera, Maggie Cardelus, Concha García, Graham Gillmore, J.Mª Guijarro, Candida Höfer, Sofía Jack, Álvaro Machimbarrena, Isidre Manils, Xisco Mensua, Angela Nordestedt, J.L. Pastor, Simeón Saiz, Carlos Schwartz, Ignacio Tovar, Oriol Vilapuig, J.M. Vela. *M* Chueca **Map p. 103, D3**

Galería Buades *Gran Vía 16, T 91 522 2562*. Quite a mix of styles here, in a gallery that sets itself the task of rooting out and displaying talented young artists, whether their genre be painting, photography or sculpture. Regulars include Ricardo Cadenas, Gennaro Castellano, Alonso Gil, Marina Núñez, June Papineau, Gonzalo Puch and MP&MP Rosado. *M* Sevilla **Map p. 8, A2**

Galería La Caja Negra *C/Fernando VI 17 (second floor), T 91 310 4360*. Graphic art and contemporary prints with changing exhibitions, from names such as Victor Mira, Robert Motherwell, Félix Curto, and Blanco Nuñez. *M* Alonso Martínez **Map p. 103, D3**

Galería del Cisne *Paseo de Eduardo Dato 17, T 91 310 0722*. Deals especially with artists from Catalonia. Artists include Julian Grau Santos, Rafael Durán, Bosco Martí, Ortuño, Moscardó, Javier Blanch, Pichot and Gloria Muñoz. *M* Rubén Darío **Map p. 103, B4**

Galería Elvira González *C/General Castaños 9, T 91 319 5900 www.galeriaelviragonzalez.com*. Contemporary Spanish minimalists, plus modern art big names, including the likes of Picasso, Calder, Chillida and Léger. If the art's too pricey you can console yourself with a print. *M* Colón **Map p. 103, D3**

Galería Juana de Aizpuru *C/Barquillo 44 (1st floor, on right), T 91 310 5561*. A key mover behind the annual art fair ARCO, and an important promoter of Spanish art on the international stage, Juana de Aizpuru opened her fist gallery in Madrid in 1970. She works with established names such as Sol LeWitt, Carlos Pazos and Dora García, as well as with newly emerging artists. *M* Chueca **Map p. 103, D3**

Galería Soledad Lorenzo *C/Orfila 5, T 91 308 2887*. Highly esteemed gallery featuring works from a broad range of contemporary artistic genres. Works mainly with established Spanish and foreign artists, including Tàpies, Ross Bleckner, Broto, Anish Kapoor, Louise Bourgeois, Victoria Civera, Georges Condo, Marta Cárdenas, Eric Fischl and Jorge

Galindo as well as Basques Txomin Badiola, Sergio Prego and Pello Izaru. *M* Alonso Martínez **Map p. 103, C4**

Max Estrella *C/Santo Tomé 6, T 91 319 5517*. Promoter of upcoming and established innovative artists, including Javier Arce, Amador, Fernando Bellver, Eugenio Cano, Pedro Castrortega, Florentino Díaz, Javier de Juan, Andrés Nagel, Miquel Navarro, Fernando Sinaga, Eduardo Vega de Seoane, Charles Sandison, Carlos Vidal and Daniel Verbis. *M* Chueca/Colón **Map p. 103, D3**

Moriarty *C/Almirante 5, T 91 5314365*. Lola Moriarty was a champion of the Movida arts scene (*see box*) and continues to deal with the avant-garde and modern art. Works by García Alix, Pérez Villalta, Ouka Lele, Paloma Muñoz, Chema Prado, Cosme Churruca and Antoni Marqués. *M* Chueca **Map p. 103, D3**

La Movida

La Movida might have come and gone, but few would dispute that 'the Movement' of the late 70s and early 80s changed the face of Madrid's cultural life for good, transforming the Spanish capital from something of a backwater into one of the most happening places in Europe. Pedro Almodóvar, actor Antonio Banderas, and a host of forward-looking designers, all contributed to washing away the drabness of the Franco era. This went right up to the city hall as Socialist mayor Enrique Tierno Galván backed a large number of cultural initiatives to the hilt. As the Movida has grown old, and some of its initiators have encountered world stardom, those heady days of the 1980s seem a little distant. The next generations haven't partied quite as hard, and the nightlife has somewhat slowed, as the pace just couldn't be kept up. Like all movements it had its day, and it had to come to an end—but it certainly left an indelible mark.

Marlborough *C/Orfila 5, T 91 319 1414*. Famous international gallery, founded in London in 1949, and focusing on the more famous artists. Deals with 19th- and 20th-century paintings and sculptures. Big international and local names include Gordillo, Bacon, Chirino, Genovés, López García, Muñoz and Saura. The Madrid gallery, designed by Richard Gluckman, is something of a work of art in itself, and all the more striking given the ugly building it is located in. *M* Alonso Martínez **Map p. 103, C4**

María Martín *C/Pelayo 52, T 91 319 6873*. Specialises in Land Art, i.e. art which involves nature. Genres are mostly sculpture and photography by Spanish and foreign artists (especially Portuguese and German). Half of the exhibited artists are women. The gallery participates in the ARCO and FIAC festivals. *M* Chueca **Map p. 103, D3**

Masha Prieto *C/Belén 2, T 91 319 5371*. Small gallery that exhibits avante-garde Spanish artists, especially those who made a name for themselves in the 80s. Represents Ouka Lele, Patricia Gadea, Pablo Aizoiala and Din Matamoro. *M* Chueca **Map p. 103, D3**

Sen *C/Barquillo 43, T 91 319 1671*. Sen exhibits paintings, sculptures and photography by contemporary artists, both up-and-coming and established. Artists on the books include Belmonte, Berrocal, Amaya Bozal, Andrés Bonilla, Ceesepe, Costus, Chronic Equipment, Eminent Grazia, Ignacio Fortún, Carlos García Alix, Julio Juste and Julio Lavallén. Has been around since 1969, though it is strongly associated with the Movida movement of the 1980s. *M* Chueca **Map p. 103, D3**

eat

Chueca by night is a place to be seen, with some fantastic old bars and stylish restaurants. Thoroughly trendy modern bars—or some would say characterless bars—that could be right at home in Soho, are also starting to spread. Gay Chueca is warm and welcoming. Malasaña has a more studenty, down-at-heel and bohemian feel to it, and can make for a thoroughly affordable night out. There are some gems of tapas bars in the area too, and further out towards the Plaza de España there are stacks of Oriental and Asian eateries.

Unless otherwise stated restaurants are open 1pm—4pm and 9pm—midnight.

€€ La Bardemcilla *C/Augusto Figueroa 47, T 91 521 4256*. Restaurant and bar owned by the internationally known, chameleon-like character actor Javier Bardem, who rose to prominence in his native Spain in J.J. Bigas Luna's 1992 classic *Jamón, Jamón*, which also starred Penélope Cruz. No giant legs of *jamón* hanging from the ceiling of this trendy modern establishment. If you don't run into the man himself, there are quite a few pictures of him on the walls. *Menú del día* for just short of €10. **M** Chueca **Map p. 103, D3**

El Bogavante de Almirante *C/Almirante 11, T 91 532 1850*. Open every day for two sittings plus lunch on Sunday. Sumptuous red-tinged lighting out of which the giant lobsters painted on the walls eye you beadily as you devour delicious offerings of the sea (and the land) in this very trendy setting. Packed in the evenings, so phone ahead. Specialities include *arroz con bogavante* (rice with lobster) and grilled lobster. **M** Chueca **Map p. 103, D3**

Carmencita *C/Libertad 16, T 91 5316 612*. You know as soon as you eye the exterior that this place is going to be something special. Elaborately tiled, furnished with marble tables, Carmencita is a joy to the senses. A lot of fish is devoured here, and the wine flows freely as the relaxed older crowd surrenders to the delightful food: a blend of Basque and Castilian. It no longer offers set daily menus: everybody's doing that, the chef maintains. Other specialities of the house include veal meatballs, lamb mash and tripe. Not the cheapest in the neighbourhood but certainly stands out in terms of quality. They have an English menu. **M** Chueca **Map p. 103, D3**

Restaurante Momo *C/Augusto Figueroa 41, T 91 532 7162*. Now an old-established favourite for innovative cuisine at bargain prices in an arty setting, well in harmony with the area. Serves great value lunchtime menu for €8 and an evening one for €12. One of the first restaurants in the area to develop a noticeably camp atmosphere, though the place is equally welcoming to gays and straights, and office workers too. Lunchtime menu costs €10 and is guaranteed to not leave you hungry. **M** Chueca **Map p. 103, D3**

€ **El 26 de Libertad** *C/Libertad 26, T 91 522 2522*. Creative dishes in a swish and colourful setting in the heart of Chueca. Terrific value *menú del día* at €9.35, though à la carte prices rapidly soar off. Curious concoctions include piquant meatballs in fish sauce—it tastes much better than it sounds. **M** Chueca **Map p. 103, D3**

El Armario *C/San Bartolomé 7, T 91 532 8377*. A youngish gay crowd who are most certainly well out of 'the closet' (to give this restaurant its English name), plus trendy straights make this a happening to place to enjoy three courses of quality Spanish fare. **M** Chueca **Map p. 103, D2**

Casa Mingo *Paseo de la Florida 2, T 915 477918. Open from 11am to midnight every day.* Near the Puente de la Reina Victoria and the Glorieta de San Vicente, the Sidras Mingo has been serving hearty Asturian dishes washed down with the region's famed cider since 1888. The whiff of the barrelled cider hits you as soon as you enter this atmospheric institution, where bottles and barrels are racked up high to the ceiling. The card-sized menu keeps things simple, and the trademark *pollo asado entero*, which is essentially chicken roasted in cider, only comes in portions for two, though the waiter will give you a doggy bag so you yourself can

Ribeira do Miño

pack up what's left to snack on later. The waiters perform the ritual of pouring the cider from up high, and you're quite likely to get a sprinkling as he gives the cider a kick into life before you consume it. Ideal for takeouts to the nearby River Manzanares or Campo del Moro. *M* Príncipe Pío **Map p. 102, D1**

La Fromagerie Normande *C/Martín de los Heros 13, T 91 542 0146.* Decent place for lunch if you get hungry before or after the nearby Museo Cerralbo. International focus with some Spanish standards on the €9 lunch menu. *M* Ventura Rodríguez **Map p. 102, D3**

El Rincón de Pelayo *C/Pelayo 19, T 91 521 8407.* An older, predominantly gay crowd flocks to this simple but stylish establishment. Like many other good places you might have to wait for a table, though it's certainly worth it. Serving eclectic dishes from Spain's varied cuisines, the daily set menu is great value at €8.50, and the evening version is almost as good at €12. *M* Chueca **Map p. 103, D3**

Ribeira Do Miño *C/Santa Brígida 1, T 91 521 9854*. Many come for the good value stacked mixed seafood platter for two for €27, though the fish dishes are beautifully prepared: try the *bacalao* (cod) made in the classic Galician style, which flakes off beautifully (€14). Also does good Galician broth (*caldo gallego*)—an ideal starter when the cockles need warming. All this is ideally complemented by the Galician white wine from the Albariño grape at €11 a bottle, and topped off by the complementary yellowy-green Galician firewater. *M* Tribunal **Map p. 103, D2**

Tienda de Vinos (El Comunista) *C/Augusto Figueroa 35, T 91 521 7012*. Apparently once run by the man who led the communist forces in Madrid's defence, and a meeting place for the left faction even during the Franco years. The atmosphere lingers on and somewhat overpowers the food, though the Tienda de Vinos serves up a number of usually decent dishes, including the satisfying rabbit with tomato. *M* Chueca **Map p. 103, D3**

OTHER CUISINES

€€ **La Panza es Primero** *C/Libertad 33, 91 521 7640*. Full-on 'Mex Mex' dipped in superb salsas that are bound to please Mexican food buffs. With Mexican ownership, 'the belly comes first' is out to prove that the way to the heart is through the stomach. A good place for a Margarita or two, Mexican beer and—naturally—tequila. Another popular Mexican place has sprung up next door, a common happening in Madrid, where one good idea often breeds another. Even names can be directly copied if proven to be successful— though that hasn't happened in this case. *M* Chueca **Map p. 103, D3**

SNACKS & TAPAS

El Bocaito *C/Libertad 4–6, T 91 532 1219*. Authentic Andalucian tapas, such as the old favourite of fried fish, in a reassuringly busy setting. Apparently a favoured hangout of the legendary film director Pedro Almodóvar. Decked out with bullfighting posters. *M* Chueca/Banco de España **Map p. 103, D3**

El Cangrejero *C/Amaniel 25, T 91 548 39 35*. As the name suggests (it means the crab-seller), the focus here is on seafood tapas. *M* Noviciado **Map p. 102, D4**

Colby *C/Barquillo 26 (corner of C/Almirante), T 91 531 0927 and C/Fuencarral 52, T 91 521 2554*. Stylish, orange-walled café-cum-restaurant chain, for some reason named after the 1980s American TV series The Colbys—which becomes apparent as soon as you look at the menu, full of fry-ups, toasts, pizza and pasta. Perfect for getting you through the working day. There's also a Colby drinks bar at C/Vergara 12. *M* Chueca **Map p. 103, D3 & 103, D2**

El Jardín Secreto *C/Conde Duque 2*. Trendy but intimate evening spot where the game is to spoil guests rotten with goodies from far-flung climes. Close to the Museum of Contemporary Art. *M* Ventura Rodríguez **Map p. 102, C4**

El Maño *C/Palma 64, T 91 521 5057*. Creative tapas such as *patatas mañas*, *canapés de cabrales con salmón*, and various others in a relaxed and comfortable setting. Good draught beer and a strong selection of house wines. *M* Noviciado **Map p. 103, C1**

La Nueva *C/Arapiles 7, T 91 447 9592*. Tapas bar steeped in atmosphere of bygone days. Its specialities include *bacalao rebozado*—cod in breadcrumbs—and *la chistorra*, sausage with

La Nueva

paprika, which hails from the northern province of Navarra. Opened in 1910. *M* Quevedo **Map p. 103, B1**

El Pez Gordo *C/Pez 6, T 91 522 3208*. The thoroughly down-to-earth 'fat fish' is known for its warm welcome, for pulling a fine pint of beer, and for its creative tapas, such as its signature dish *migas*, a variation on the Aragonese offering of breadcrumbs fried deliciously in olive oil with grapes, green pepper and sausage. A hangout for trendy locals, though it never feels unwelcoming. *M* Noviciado **Map p. 103, D1**

Stop Madrid *C/Hortaleza 11, T 91 521 8887*. One of those classic old bars and tapas joints with wines stacked high to the ceiling and a broad choice of beers to accompany tapas staples like *boquerones* and portions of *jamón*. Quite simply, well worth a stop. *M* Chueca **Map p. 103, D2**

BARS & NIGHTLIFE

Café la Palma *C/Palma 62, T 91 522 5031*. Trendy nightspot that packs a lot in to its relatively compact dimensions, playing host to regular live music as well as international DJs. Several distinct rooms, including one in with incredibly low seating on cushions that encourages patrons to stretch out. *M* Noviciado **Map p. 103, C1**

Café Pepe Botella *C/San Andrés 12 (Plaza Dos de Mayo), T 91 522 4309*. Studenty/arty hangout though welcoming to all comers. Just the place to settle down and consult your notes over a coffee or something stronger. *M* Tribunal **Map p. 103, C1**

Libertad 8 *C/Libertad 8, T 91 539 7826*. Many of today's stars started out in the back room here, and plenty of budding pop stars still come to play. No-nonsense bar out front in this celebrated Movida hangout. *M* Chueca **Map p. 103, D3**

Museo Chicote *Gran Vía 12, T 91 532 6737*. Steeped in the atmosphere of the stars of yesteryear, and still pulling in its fair share of celebrities today, Museo Chicote is a good place to mix with the in-crowd if you're up to it. By poking you're head around the door you'll soon know if this place does it for you or not. Opened its doors in 1931 when Perico Chicote, a former barman at the Ritz, decided to go it alone. Past clients are just too famous to bother mentioning. *M* Gran Vía/Plaza de España **Map p. 8, A2**

Taberna de Ángel Sierra *C/Gravina 11, T 91 531 0126*. A real meeting point for the gay and the straight alternative crowd just as you

The Madrid attitude to nightlife: party till you drop

come out of the underground from Chueca. Revellers frequently spill out into the square outside. Defines the classic old Madrid bar look: zinc-topped bar, attractively tiled, and the *vermut* flowing freely *M* Chueca **Map p. 103, D3**

CAFÉS

Café Acualera *C/Gravina 10, T 91 522 2143*. An overtly kitsch café in absolutely the right setting. Just the place to flop in the comfy chairs after a hard night of action or even the middle of a night out. Topped off with a nude male statue. *M* Chueca **Map p. 103, D3**

Café Commercial *Glorieta de Bilbao 7, T 91 521 5655. Open 8am–1am, later at weekends*. You'll definitely be tempted to drop into this gem of a coffee house to read the papers. The place has a distinct whiff of more relaxed days, though there's Internet access upstairs should you need it. Prime location to take breakfast and thumb through the news of the day, or you could admire yourself in one of the mirrors that dominate this classic old-style, marbled café. *M* Bilbao **Map p. 103, C2**

shop

A new generation of alterative designers has sprung up in Chueca, especially on Calle Almirante and the surrounding streets, and in Malasaña they offer a cutting edge alternative to the big boys and girls of the Salamanca area. Calle Fuencarral is stacked with stores with even funkier and yet more affordable clothes, and accessory stores pitched at the clubbing generation. There's even a several-level indoor market dedicated to putting together the most distinctive of outfits.

ACCESSORIES

Mercado Fuencarral *C/Fuencarral 45. Open Mon–Sat 10am–9pm*. A four-level bazaar in the thick of Malasaña's with-it shopping area, and very much geared to dressing up and rounding off the outfits of the hippest of the club-goers with a slightly grungy veneer. Among the plethora of stores and stalls is the rather lamely-named Trendy, which sells striking and relatively inexpensive jewellery from renowned Catalan designer Carles Galindo. Music store AMA can provide some real surprises, while gallery Espacio F hosts art that suits the happening backdrop. The basement bar is the hangout of party goers in their pre-going out mode. *M* Tribunal **Map p. 103, D2**

CLOTHES

Ararat *C/Conde de Xiquena 13 and C/Almirante 10 & 11*. Top local and Spanish creations at these three shops featuring competitively priced and eye-catching going-out gear. Men catered for at C/Conde Xiquena, women at C/Almirante. *M* Chueca **Map for both p. 103, D3**

Arena *C/Conde de Xiquena 7*. Noted Spanish designers and international designers David Delfín, Roberto Diaz. José Miró, Miriam Ponsa, Amaya Arzuaga, Vivienne Westwood and Versace. Arena acts as an outlet for its international stuff with prices slashed by up to 7%. *M* Chueca/Banco de España **Map p. 103, D3**

Bdba *C/Fuencarral 48*. Enticing party frocks and day wear for women from mainly Spanish designers at competitive prices. Also has some clothes from the US. *M* Tribunal **Map p. 103, D2**

The Catwalk 1 *C/Almirante 6*. Italian and Brazilian designer labels with shoes from Spain's Clara García. *M* Chueca **Map p. 103, D3**

Custo Barcelona *C/Fuencarral 29*. The quirky T-shirt empire created by Barcelona's Custo Dalmau continues to make not-so-basic T-shirts that stand out from the pack. Also sells similarly innovative accessories and shoes for both sexes. Also at C/Major 37 and Claudio Coello 91. *M* Chueca/Gran Vía **Map p. 8, A2 (contd. from p. 103, D2)**

The Deli Room *C/Santa Bárbara 4*. Bright and cheery designs from alternative Spanish designers, both professional and amateur, in the bizarre setting of a deli store. Shoes are even placed where cheese and meats would normally go! *M* Tribunal **Map p. 103, D2**

Doble AA *C/Fuencarral 31*. If you neither have the inclination nor financial clout to fork out on designer clothes but like to dress somewhat differently or eccentrically, visit one of the four Doble AA shops offering more than a dozen different brands ranging from Miss Sixty and DKNY to Custo. Jeans, shoes, bags and accessories—all in one place to compile a season's wardrobe. Branches: Mercado de Fuencarral 45, ABC Serrano 61, Príncipe de Vergara 22. *M* Tribunal **Map p. 8, A2 (contd. from p. 103, D2)**

Fun & Basics *C/Fuencarral 43*. Spanish company dealing in shoes and a host of accessories. Classy design at very good prices. Also offers snazzy gloves, wallets, purses, umbrellas, scarves, hats, jewellery and luggage. It has nine shops and counting in Madrid. *M* Tribunal **Map p. 103, D2**

Helena Valtierra *C/Santa Bárbara 9*. Bright and colourful retro clothes with a bit of a rustic-cum-oriental touch. The same goes for the accessories. *M* Tribunal **Map p. 103, D2**

Loreak Mendian *C/ Argensola 5*. Now's your chance to stock up on must-have items from this popular Basque label, the ultimate in metropolitan style—and entirely unavailable outside Spain. *M* Alonso Martínez, **Map p. 103, D3**

Mi lolita shoes and more... *C/Almirante 11*. Seductively angled stilettos, pointed, rounded, whichever way you like it, with these almost artistic shoes from Spanish shoemakers Paco Gil and Victorio & Lucchino. *M* Chueca **Map p. 103, D3**

Mitsuoko *C/Fuencarral 59*. Not Japanese as it may sound, but rather a very 'in' Spanish label that caters for both sexes with flash designs owing a lot to the some of the more cutting-edge styles of recent decades. Has just the café to go with the store. *M* Tribunal **Map p. 103, D2**

Momo *C/Almirante 8*. Warm colours and soft pinks abound. Also at C/Jorge Juan 14. *M* Chueca **Map p. 103, D3**

Paco Racionero *C/Almirante 5*. Elegant (and for that read *elegant*—not boring) evening wear for the mature woman, plus other labels. *M* Chueca **Map p. 103, D3**

HOME AND DESIGN

Casa Julia *C/Almirante 1*. Three levels of an eclectic mix of coffee tables, bedsteads, oriental clothes, and various bric-à-brac, with lots of smaller stuff that's easier to take home as well—you might have a problem shifting the Romanesque columns. Jewellery too. The steep wonky steps add to the ambience of the place. *M* Chueca **Map p. 103, D3**

JEWELLERY

Complemento Directo *C/Augusto Figueroa 35*. Alternative jewellery designs from Amparo de la Concepción using semi-precious stones, glass, wood and ceramics, plus very snazzy T-shirts and pashmina shawls. Also offers custom-made jewellery. *M* Chueca **Map p. 103, D3**

Fariña & Almuzara *C/Conde de Xiquena 12*. Unique and luxurious jewellery and gems created exclusively from Fariña & Almuzara's handsome designs. *M* Chueca **Map p. 103, D3**

LINGERIE

Blonda Lenceria *C/Orellana 3*. Discreet store offering sumptuous lingerie from the likes of Andrés Sarda, Lise Charmel, Verde Veronica and Épris de Lise Charmel. *M* Alonso Martínez/Colón **Map p. 103, C3**

FOOD

Cacao Sampaka *C/Orellana 4*. This modern shop-cum-café is definitely one for chocolate addicts everywhere, with its superb and well-presented selection of all things chocolate. For those who want to take their addiction further, there are books on the history of chocolate, and a range of international sweet wines to round off your experience. **M** Alonso Martínez/Colón **Map p. 103, C3**

Niza Manuel Vaquero *C/Argensola 24*. Gorgeous bijou *pastelería* with a tempting range of cakes, sweets and pastry on offer. The wooden design inside resembles a wedding cake, encased by the dark wood and marble exterior. **M** Alonso Martínez/Colón **Map p. 103, D3**

Patrimonio Comunal Olivarero *C/Mejía Lequerica 1*. 150 brands of extra virgin olive oil on offer from this association of olive oil makers that's out to preach the benefits and get us to take up using the healthy oil—as if they need to. Just like wines, the oils are classified by region. **M** Alonso Martínez **Map p. 103, D3**

SHOES

111 *C/Piamonte 27*. Hip urban footwear in a stylish showroom. Also makes customized footwear. **M** Alonso Martínez/Chueca **Map p. 103, D3**

Enola *C/Barquillo 18*. Quirky and classy shoes and boots from Pedro García, Jaime Mascaró and his daughter Ursula, plus El Naturalista. Also attractive Italian bags. **M** Chueca **Map p. 103, D3**

Kassen Zapata *C/Barquillo 26*. 60s-inspired shoes and boots for both men and women. Also eye-catching bags, hats, accessories, gloves and jewellery. **M** Chueca **Map p. 103, D3**

SPECIALIST

Crisis Cómics *C/Luna 28*. Vast and colourful selection of comics and other publications. **M** Noviciado **Map p. 103, D1**

Equus Riding Shop *C/Hilarión Eslava 32*. Devoted to all things equestrian, for professionals and amateurs alike. Deals in clothes from Aigle and La Martina, and saddles and leather accessories from Devoucoux and Macel. **M** Moncloa/Argüelles **Map p. 102, B3**

Naipe Juegos *C/Meléndez Valdés 55*. Superb collection of games from all around the world. All the old classics and many new themed games, plus accessories for bridge. **M** Argüelles/Moncloa **Map p. 102, B3**

STATIONERY/WRITING

Palmapapel *C/Palma 34*. Lavish selection of paper from all over the world, most of it almost too good to write on or wrap presents in. *M* Tribunal/Noviciado **Map p. 103, C1**

Sancer *C/Fernández de los Ríos 93*. Technical stationery shop for artists, architects, fashion designers, decorative artists. Handy if your trip to Madrid should inspire creative impulses. *M* Moncloa **Map p. 102, B3**

WINE

Bodega de los Reyes *C/Reyes 6. Open 10.30am–2.30 pm and then again from 5.15pm–9pm evenings on weekdays and 11am–2.30pm on Saturdays.* Well presented selection of Spanish and foreign wines with welcoming service in this compact but well stocked bodega. *M* Noviciado **Map p. 102, D4**

Reserva y Cata *C/Conde de Xiquena 13*. Rapidly growing wine merchants with seven intimate shops in Madrid, all with very welcoming service. They stock a wide range of Spanish and international wines to suit all pockets. Even the cheap stuff is good quality. They've also launched their own wines, bottled to their requirements by producers they deal with, all perfect examples of immensely drinkable modern Spanish wines. *M* Chueca/Colón **Map p. 103, D3**

SALAMANCA, RECOLETOS & UP THE CASTELLANA

As chic and as exclusive as Spain gets, the grid of streets known as Salamanca, stamping ground of the *'picos'* and *'picas'*—the stylish young things—is filled with places to offload your hard-earned cash—and you won't have to go far to do this. Salamanca is home to some of the biggest names in Spanish fashion. The top-flight designers tend to take up shop around the corner of C/Serrano and C/Ortega y Gasset, while as Serrano is crossed by C/Goya the scene turns to the more affordable retail stores. It's not all shopping, though. For those prepared to give up retail for an afternoon, there is also a relatively unknown art treasure tucked away (the Museo Lázaro Galdiano—quite a trek, but worth it). Art galleries stacked with unsurprisingly pricey art works abound in the sidestreets.

Museo Lázaro Galdiano

OPEN	Weds–Mon 10am–4.30pm
CLOSED	Tuesday
CHARGES	€4; €3 reduced admission. Free on Wednesdays. Closed 1/1, Maundy Thursday, Good Friday, 1/6, 2/6, 1/11, 6/12, 25/12
TELEPHONE	91 561 6084
WEB	www.flg.es
ENTRANCE	C/Serrano 122
DISABLED ACCESS	No
METRO	Rubén Darío/Gregorio Marañón
SERVICES	Small shop with items from the museum

HIGHLIGHTS

Works by Goya

This gem of a collection of fine art is well worth seeking out, as it has striking pieces from big Spanish names such as Goya, Zurbarán, Murillo and El Greco (well, he adopted Spain), as well as Flemish masters Bosch and Teniers, and a miniature work by Constable.

The collection once belonged to the Spanish intellectual and financier José Lázaro Galdiano, a Navarran who regarded the collection of Spanish art as the key to tracing the nation's identity. He bequeathed his hoard to the state on his death in 1947. On top of the paintings, the Lázaro Galdiano also houses many sculptures, jewellery, ceramics, and other objets d'art, the earliest dating from the 4th century BC. The collection is spread over three floors.

FIRST FLOOR
The most notable works are El Greco's *Adoration of the Magi* and Zurbarán's *San Diego de Alcalá (pictured overleaf)* Both hang in room 2 towards the right-hand corner.

SECOND FLOOR
This is where the collection really gets going, with a marvellous ornate bench from Cuenca [7]. There are also a number of works attributed to Goya or followers of Goya [13], and the debate goes on to this day as to whether the master really did lend them his paintbrush. The museum admits that there is some dissent on the part of critics that as to their authenticity. However, it maintains that their quality suggests that they are indeed by the master, and that until research proves otherwise they will hang as Goyas. Judge for yourself, and contrast them with the works in the adjoining Goya Cabinet Room [G.I], about whose attribution there's no question. The painting on the opposite wall as you enter, known both as *The Spell* and *The Witches*, contains amazing detail for such a small painting in the grotesque faces portrayed.

MUSEO LÁZARO GALDIANO
SECOND FLOOR

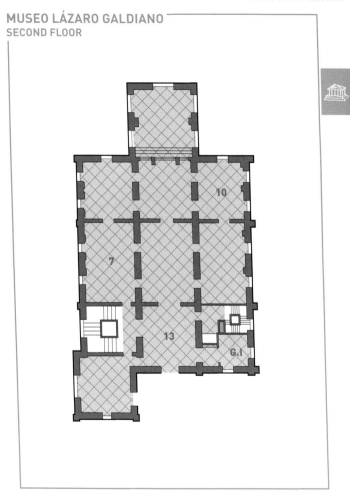

Francisco de Zurbarán: *San Diego de Alcalá* (undated: 17th century)

Next to it hangs the similarly pint-sized *Witches' Sabbath*, where decidedly unearthly figures carry out a bizarre ritual. Both are from either 1797 or 1798. A year or so later Goya painted *St Hermengild in Prison*, which occupies the opposite wall. A sense of the saint's confinement is brilliantly emphasized by Goya's use of light. Between them hang four Goya sketches. For something a bit brighter and more breezy there's *La Era* ('The Threshing Floor', 1786), one of Goya's classic country scenes.

El Greco's spooky and repentant *St Francis of Assisi* is a must-see [10], with Murillo's *St Rose of Lima* and works by Zurbarán and José de Ribera hanging alongside it.

THIRD FLOOR

In Room 17, on the right hand side towards the back, there's Bosch's superb *Meditation of St John the Baptist*. More subtle than some of his best known pieces, the abnormal flora and fauna that almost envelop the saint imply a somewhat unsettled mind and evoke the usual Bosch focus on the surreal. Look out too for Cranach's distinctive *Christ Child Triumphant over Death and Sin*, and Jan Brueghel's take on *The Animals Entering Noah's Ark*—all taking place in a contemporary Flemish setting. Room 19 houses a number of works from the British School from the 17th–19th centuries, including Constable's *The Road from East Bergholt to Flatford*.

Museo Sorolla

OPEN	Tues–Sat 9.30am–3pm, Sun and holidays 10am–3pm
CLOSED	Mondays
CHARGES	€2.40; €1.5 reduced admission. Free on Sundays, 18/5, 12/10, 6/12. Concessions available
TELEPHONE	91 310 1584

WEB   www.museosorolla.mcu.es
ENTRANCE   Paseo del General Martínez Campos 37
METRO   Rubén Darío

HIGHLIGHTS

The White Slave Trade
The Pink Bathrobe
Strolling along the Seashore

Museo Sorolla is the one-time home and centre of creativity of Spain's very own impressionist heavyweight, Joaquín Sorolla Bastida (1863–1923), whose works are exhibited in four rooms that remain very much as they were in his day. Aside from his paintings, the museum is replete with Sorolla's furniture and personal belongings, and the surrounding gardens are a delight.

A renowned and internationally celebrated painter in his day, Sorolla, who hailed from Valencia, did not enjoy posthumous success, and is today a relatively unknown name. And yet, though you may not know his name, you'll find that you have seen some of these images before.

Sorolla's former home, which is straight out of Andalucia in terms of its design, has exhibited his work since 1925, after the bequest of Sorolla's widow Clotilde García del Castillo. Her portrait hangs in the first room. The museum was built in 1911 by the architect Enrique María de Repullés y Vargas, to designs overseen by Sorolla himself. Sorolla certainly had a hand in designing the Andalucian garden.

The museum has recently undergone an impressive restoration restoring it to all its former glory, so that today the Museo Sorolla is a veritable oasis of peace and tranquillity amid a bustling city.

The exhibit starts in three interlocking rooms [I, II and III], which were Sorolla's work and exhibition area. In the first room is Sorolla's hard-hitting early piece *The White Slave Trade* [I], painted in 1894 during his Social Realism phase. It depicts rounded-up

MUSEO SOROLLA
GROUND FLOOR

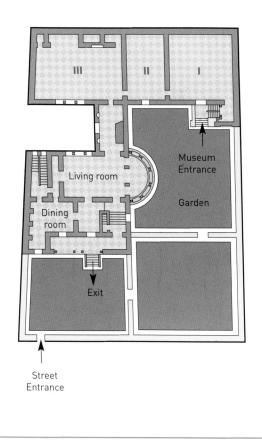

III II I

Museum
Entrance

Living room

Garden

Dining
room

Exit

Street
Entrance

Joaquín Sorolla: *Strolling along the Seashore* (1909)

country girls being taken to market, in this case a brothel, watched over by the *celestina* or procuress. Later Sorolla works become brighter and less sullen as he begins to experiment with *luminismo*, a style whereby the quality of the light is rendered somehow more intense than that of the Impressionists, perfectly capturing the piercing sunshine of his native Valencia.

The next room [II] is especially noteworthy for *The Pink Bathrobe*. Painted in Valencia in the summer of 1916, it is a stunning example of the *luminismo* style: a woman is being dressed in a light housecoat with light streaming in from several sources.

The beautifully fluent and graceful *Strolling along the Seashore* from 1909 [III] is perhaps the most recognisable of Sorolla's works, and features his wife and elder daughter clad in white dresses and draperies flapping in the breeze.

Upstairs in Room IV is *Snapshot, Biarritz*, which was painted in summer 1906 at the French beach resort where Sorolla went via a couple of months in Paris. It can be seen in this one of his early Impressionist works. In *Siesta*, painted in 1911, his brushstrokes are so deeply engraved that they almost seem carved out of the canvas.

Also on show are Sorolla's own collections ranging from ancient and modern sculpture and furniture to gold, precious objects and a painstakingly assembled collection of Spanish ceramics, mainly from Valencia and Aragón. There are also various sketches and gouaches on display.

Before heading back to modern Madrid, you might want to spend a few minutes of quiet reflection in the relaxing Andalucian garden.

Museo de Escultura al Aire Libre de la Castellana

(CASTELLANA OPEN-AIR SCULPTURE MUSEUM)

OPEN	Round the clock
CHARGES	None
ENTRANCE	Paseo de la Castellana 41
DISABLED ACCESS	Yes
METRO	Rubén Darío

Tucked away under the flyover connecting Calle Juan Bravo and Paseo Eduardo Dato that passes over Madrid's great north road, the Castellana, this museum might go unnoticed at first. In fact locals wander past and walk through the site without batting an eyelid at some of the work on show, no matter how famous the hands that fashioned it, or how hard it tries to arrest the attention. This is one museum that's accessible 24/7 and has been open continuously since 1979, featuring the different trends within the Spanish abstract sculpture movement.

The 17 works, the majority of which were crafted by members of the post-Civil War abstract movement, all show contrasting styles. Nevertheless they blend in nicely with the modern urban surroundings—the flyover, the concrete steps and the pedestrian crossing—which certainly appears to have been the aim of the site's planners. The waterfall, which highlights Martín Chirino's bright red *Mediterránea*, also serves to dampen the noise of the roaring traffic. Spain's first attempts to break out of the traditional mode are represented by the legendary Catalan artist Joan Miró's penguin-like bronze *Mère Ubu*, and works by other members of the avant-garde Julio González and Alberto Sánchez.

The work of Gabino, Leoz, Palazuelo, Rueda, Torner and Alfaro can be characterized by a focus on geometrical shapes. Rivera maximises the use of light, Chirino, Serrano, Chillida and Martí seek expression in volumes and the materials they use, while Subirach and Sempere opt for expression in movement. Serrano's *Unidades-Yunta* is located across the road. The railings, benches, the fountain and the lighting were designed by Sempere. All the sculptures were donated by the artists themselves or by their relatives.

in the area

Museo Arqueológico Nacional *C/Serrano 13, T 91 577 7912. Open Tues–Sat 9.30am–8.30pm, Sun and holidays 9.30am–2.30pm. www.man.es* Comprehensive collection of artifacts covering civilisations that have existed in Spain from the prehistoric through Iberian tribes, to Roman occupation, the Visigoths and Moorish conquests. The museum is especially notable for a copy of the famous prehistoric cave paintings from Cantabria, arches from Zaragoza's Aljafería palace, and Roman mosaics. Wander around and it soon becomes obvious that artistic expression isn't anything new in Spain. *M* Colón **Map p. 132, D2–C2**

Museo de la Ciudad *C/Príncipe de Vergara 140, T 91 588 6599 Free admission.* With its focus on the development of the city's utilities and transport, this museum is strictly for off-duty telecoms experts, engineers and town planners. *M* Cruz del Rayo **Map pp. 2–3**

Palacio de Correos y Comunicaciones *C/Montalbán, T 91 396 2000. Open Mon–Fri 9am–2pm and 5pm–7pm, Sat 10am–1.30pm.* This palatial building, which is in fact the central Post Office, overlooks the impressive Plaza de la Cibeles. It was built between 1906 and 1919 and is similarly plush on the inside. It's definitely worth taking a look in.

It also houses a free museum with stamps from all over the globe and exhibits on the history of communications. *M* Banco de España **Map p. 132, D1**

Puerta de Alcalá One of the city's defining monuments, designed by Francesco Sabatini, who was employed by Carlos III to take Madrid into the modern, Neoclassical, world. *M* Retiro **Map p. 132, D2**

Puerta de Europa *Plaza de Castilla.* These architecturally striking twin towers that have leaned imperiously over the Paseo de la Castellana, Madrid's northern vein, since 1996, are the world's first leaning high-rise buildings—listing, as opposed to listed.

Located at the northern end of the business district, they symbolically represent a gateway to Europe, which also happens to be their name. Puerta de Europa came into being as a major office and residential project, where the location of the site directly over a underground interchange rendered it structurally impossible for the buildings to be built near the street. Thus, for the two towers of 114 metres in height to be considered as twin towers, John Burgee Architects along with Philip Johnson made them lean towards each other. *M* Plaza de Castilla **Map pp. 2–3**

commercial galleries

Alcolea *C/Velázquez 12, T 91 435 2347*. Contemporary and traditional paintings including Impressionist landscape art by established painters and newcomers. Artists exhibited include Aguilar Moré, Casaus Canadells, Isidoro Lázaro, Isidro Cistaré, Manuel Blesa and Joan Martí. *M* Velázquez **Map p. 132, C2**

Atalante Tapices *Plaza de la Independencia 4, T 91 426 1270*. Belgian tapestry buyer turned seller Charles Rifon and his wife Luz de Val run this gallery which is devoted solely to tapestry from the 15th C to the present with British, Italian, French, Belgian and Spanish tapestry represented. A tapestry from Goya might cost €60,000—which is at least a hundred times cheaper than one of his paintings. Other tapestries start at €10,000 and go up to €250,000. Atalante also carries out restoration of tapestries, textiles and carpets. *M* Retiro **Map p.132, D2**

Capa Esculturas *C/Claudio Coello 19, T 91 431 0365*. Owned by Eduardo Capa, this gallery displays some striking modern works from young Spanish sculptors, plus a few established names such as Ignacio Asenjo Salcedo, who creates highly colourful sculptures working primarily with plastics. Prices range from €120–€140 for series numbering over 1,500; multiples of 75 pieces range from €319–€500, while originals of eight pieces range from €600–€2,400. *M* Retiro/Serrano **Map p. 132, D2**

Egam *C/Villanueva 29, T 91 435 31 61*. Open since 1969, this highly rated gallery specializes in all forms of contemporary art from the younger generation, covering the abstract to realism through various art forms. Regulars include Alcaín, Almela, Aparicio, Nati Bermejo, Cardenes, Feito, Amparo Garrido, Pedro Morales, Montserrat Gómez Osuna and Carmen Laffón. **M** Retiro **Map p. 132, D2**

Galería 57 *C/Columela 3, T 91 577 5397.* Abstract painting, sculpture and photography from Spanish and foreign contemporary artists, with some focus on minimalist and conceptual art. Artists exhibited include Pedro Castrortega, Nikola Dimitrov, Luis Cruz Hernández, Lotje de Lussannet, Juan Sotomayor, Óscar Seco, Yurihito Otsuki, Alfonso Sicilia Sobrino, Maurizio Lanzillotta and Pilar Lara. **M** Retiro **Map p. 132, D2**

Galería Durán *C/Serrano 30, T 91 431 6605.* Painting and sculpture at this gallery seeks to show realism in all its forms. Exhibiting artists include Eustaqui Segrelles, Faustino Manchado, Adolfo Estrada, Hernández Cop, Santos Hu, Iglesias Sanz and Paz Figares (sculpture). Galería Durán is unique in that it runs a biennial national painting competition open to pros and amateurs alike. **M** Serrano **Map p. 132, C2**

Galería Fernando Pradilla *C/Claudio Coello 20, T 91 575 4804.* A showcase for Latin-American, Spanish and international art, through artists directly represented by the gallery itself or in collaboration with some major Latin American galleries. Artists include Ana Adarve, Salvador Diaz, Juan Gallego, Vicky Neumann, Jorge Ortega and Ambra Polidori. Pradilla opened his first gallery in Bogota, Colombia in 1987, and set up shop in Madrid in 2001. **M** Retiro **Map p. 132, D2**

Galería Guillermo de Osma *C/Claudio Coello 4, T 91 435 59 36.* The place to find avant-garde works from between 1910 and 1940. Worth calling ahead to check opening hours. **M** Retiro **Map p. 132, D2**

Galería Metta *C/Villanueva 36, T 91 576 8141.* Paintings, graphic art, drawings and photography from upcoming Spanish artists. This is also a showcase for foreign artists in Madrid. Metta deals with names such as Aillaud, David Nash, and Larry Poons, and Ràfols-Casamada. **M** Príncipe de Vergara **Map p. 132, D2**

Jovenart *C/Claudio Coello 16, 21 & 22, T 91 431 9828.* As its name suggests, this gallery acts as a showcase for younger, upcoming artists. These include many Spanish names, though international painters are central to the collection: Frank Jensen from Denmark, Monika from Estonia, Mersad Berber from Croatia and Carlos Meide from Argentina. Prices ranges from €150 to €12,000 a painting. **M** Retiro/Serrano **Map p. 132, D2**

Joyería Ansorena, *C/Alcalá 42, 54, C/Alfonso XI 2, T 91 532 8515.* Founded in 1845, the Ansorena hosts up to 1,230 works of art in three separate spaces covering many styles of painting, furniture, carpets and even church furniture. It holds three auctions every month, usually towards the middle of the month. *M* Retiro/Banco de España **Map p. 132, D1; p. 8, A3; p. 132, D1**

Oliva Arauna *C/Claudio Coello 19, T 91 4351808.* Since 1979 this gallery and art bookshop has been dedicated to graphic art. Works are by Lucio Muñoz, José Hernández, Manuel Alcorlo, Antoni Abad, Chema Alvargonzález, Per Barclay, Christophe Boutin, José Herrera, Alicia Martín, Christian Philipp Müller and Miguel Río Branco among others. They also organize talks. Technology is used to the full to display this varied bag. *M* Retiro **Map p. 132, D2**

Peccato Veniale *C/Conde de Aranda 20, T 91 426 0378.* Gallery-cum-clothes shop where you can stop off for a drink. *M* Retiro **Map p. 132, D2**

Pheo *C/Recoletos 15, T 91 5755 474.* Felipe González—though not the former PM—deals with young Spanish artists such as Mersuka Dopazo and Antonio Castor. *M* Retiro **Map p. 132, D1**

Rafael García Arte Galería *Plaza de la Independencia 10, T 91 521 5412.* Overlooking the Puerta de Alcalá, Rafael García houses temporary paintings from Spanish artists, including from the minimalist Benito Lozano. Aside from the temporary displays, a host of sculptures, decorations, furniture and other paintings are on display in an exhibition space to the right of the entrance. *M* Retiro **Map p. 132, D2**

Supermercado de Arte *C/Serrano 4.* A commercial gallery with a difference. Art is a commodity just like any other product and the Art Supermarket's new year sale (late November to early January) takes an everything-must-go approach with prints ranging from €79 to €229. Works from names such as Pilar Tarifa, Març Rabal, Martín Burguillo, Helena de la Guardia, Montesol, P.G, Pedro Epasa and Rafael Arjona. *M* Retiro **Map p. 132, D2**

Theo *C/Marqués de la Ensenada 2, T 91 308 23 59.* Theo has been selling major works of art since the dark days of Franco, and is amongst the oldest galleries in Madrid. In its time it has served to showcase work from many of Spain's exiled artists, including Picasso. Artists represented today include Arp, Calder, Tàpies, Soto, and Picasso. Also deals with foreign artists. *M* Colón **Map p. 132, C1**

Tórculo *C/Claudio Coello 17, T 91 575 86 86.* Graphic art from the likes of José Hernández, Lucio Muñoz and Manuel Alcorlo. Also serves as an art bookshop. *M* Retiro/Serrano **Map p. 132, D2**

eat

Unless otherwise stated restaurants are open 1pm—4pm and 9pm—midnight.

€€€ **El Amparo** *C/de Puigcerdá 8, T 91 431 6456.* Superbly designed and one of the most fantastically creative of all Madrid's restaurants, a merging of Basque, new-style Madrid and French flair. The dishes taste as elaborate (and just as exquisite) as they sound: venison millefeuille of boletus with dewlap of Iberian pork and ragout of sea snails and ravioli stuffed with goose liver paté and truffles. Great wine list with sommelier José Miguel Fernández on hand to talk you through it. Booking essential and sometimes well ahead. *M* Serrano **Map p. 132, C2**

Pedro Larumbe *C/Serrano 61, T 91 575 1112.* Pedro Larumbe was first the chef and later the manager of Cabo Mayor, the highly acclaimed Cantabrian gourmet establishment in northern Madrid. He opened his own place here in 1996. Elegant setting, summer roof terrace and exquisite contemporary dishes from a small, regularly changing menu. Recurring favourites including warm lobster salad and a very creative cod dish: *bacalao al pil-pil verde de cilantro.* Mouth-watering as well as eye-catching desserts. Located at the top of the Andalucian-style ABC shopping centre, once the home of the ABC newspaper, between Paseo de la Castellana and Calle Serrano. *M* Serrano **Map p. 132, B2**

El Pescador *C/José Ortega y Gasset 75, T 91 402 1290. Closed Sundays.* Imaginative seafood dishes brimming with taste. The house speciality is a grilled sole dish, *lenguado Evaristo*, named after the restaurant's owner. *Salpicón de mariscos*, a salad of mixed seafood with onions in vinaigrette, is sure to get the tastebuds going. *M* Lista **Map p. 132, B4**

€€ **A Bocados** *C/Jorge Juan 70, T 91 435 8101.* Anti-establishment chef José Gorines, a disciple of the great Iñaki Izaguirre, serves up a raft of highly imaginative experimental dishes. There are sampler menus that offer a bit of each of his creations. Black and silver décor sets the mood: this is not supposed to be a restaurant where you sit back and relax. The only thing lacking is a minimalist wine list. *M* Goya **Map p. 132, C4**

Casa Carola *C/Padilla 54, T 91 401 9408*. Famed for its *cocido madrileño*, a typical Madrid dish of chick-peas, meats and veg, though made with the very finest ingredients, cooked together but served separately. They promise their food to be '*de la puta madre*'—to give a loose translation: 'motherf***ing good'. Casa Carola has recently opened a second restaurant of the same name not far from the Santiago Bernabeu stadium at C/Victor Andrés Belaúnde 6, T 91 458 3159. *M* Núñez de Balboa **Map p. 132, B4**

OTHER CUISINES

€€ **Al-Mounia** *C/Recoletos 5, T 91 435 0828*. Atmospheric, refined and highly authentic Moroccan restaurant in Casbah setting, where the music, the painted ceiling and the low round tables set the scene. Trademark dishes include *meshoui* (barbecued lamb), but this works as a place to sit and relax too, over a cup of tea in the tearoom next door. If you're one of those intent only on sampling local cuisine when on holiday, then you might bend to include Al-Mounia given the influence North Africa has exerted on Spanish development over the millennia. *M* Retiro **Map p. 132, D1**

Mumbai Massala *C/Recoletos 14, T 91 435 7194*. Authentic Indian restaurant, though the dishes tend to be not that spicy. *M* Retiro **Map p. 132, D1**

TAPAS

Finos y Finas *C/Espartinas 6, T 91 575 9069*. Swish sherry bar with creative tapas. *M* Príncipe de Vergara/Goya **Map p. 132, C3**

José Luis *C/Serrano 89, T 91 5630958*. Open from lunchtime to after midnight. One of the doyens of the tapas scene. It's hardly worth picking on any individual dish as it's all so good—but here goes anyway: how about smoked salmon tartare, spanish omelette, grilled pork loin, marinated anchovies (*boquerones en vinagre*). The list isn't endless, but it sure goes on and on. *M* Núñez de Balboa **Map p. 132, A2**

CAFÉS

Café Gijón *Paseo de Recoletos 21, T 91 521 5425*. Classic old café opened in 1888 by Gumersindo Gómez, and now forever linked to the literary set. Patrons have included Federico García Lorca, Rafael Alberti and Pablo Neruda, who all used to hang out here together in the 1920s. Nowadays the service leaves quite a lot to be desired, though the terrace is an absolute picture in summer. A long established favourite for *tertulias*—lively but civilised debate. The tables are given over to lunch from noon to 4pm, when you won't be able to make your coffee stretch the afternoon. *M* Banco de España **Map p. 132, D1**

Café Espejo *Paseo de Recoletos 31, T 91 319 1122.* Art Nouveau pavilion—but appearances deceive. Though it looks as if it has been there almost as long as its neighbour the Café Gijón, it is in fact just 25 years old. Pleasant tiled restaurant at the back specialising in French and Basque delicacies and a *terraza* over the street in summer, to which they'll bring you great tapas. *M* Colón **Map p. 132, C1**

WINE BARS

Terrabacus Vinoteca *C/Lagasca 74, T 91 435 3718.* Smart wine bar/wine club with some 60 wines available by the glass and five times that number by the bottle. You can drop in just for a casual glass or two, or if you want to take the wine thing seriously, you can partake in themed tastings. *M* Serrano/Velázquez **Map p. 132, C2**

shop

ACCESSORIES

Scooter *Callejón de Jorge Juan.* Jewellery, handbags and sunglasses from Scooter, Vanessa Bruno, Isabel Marant, Lluis Genero-Alchemy, Helmut Lang. *M* Serrano **Map p. 132, C2**

Sun Planet *C/Goya 11.* Sunglasses galore with styles for all manner of occasions. In Madrid you certainly could do with a good pair in the summer. *M* Serrano **Map p. 132, C2**

BdeB HOME *C/Claudio Coello 17.* Just the place for finding that elusive wedding gift, from this collection of exclusive linen, crystal ware, colourful cushions and other interior decoration: might be a bit tricky to lug home, though. *M* Retiro **Map p. 132, D2**

CLOTHES

Adolfo Domínguez *C/José Ortega y Gasset 4 & C/Serrano 96*. Domínguez's functional and relaxed designs define classic Spanish fashion. Aimed at a wide public of men and women everywhere. Reasonable prices for quality design with suits starting at around €300. Also does good-value lines of lingerie, perfumes, shoes, jewellery and various accessories. The Ortega y Gasset branch has women's items only. Serrano branch is open all day. *M* Serrano **Map p. 132, B2 for both**

Carolina Herrera *C/Serrano 16*. The renowned Venezuelan designer's Madrid branch. The shop itself is beautifully laid out, with a bar and a pool table (only decorative, unfortunately). *M* Serrano **Map p. 132, D2**

Sybilla *Callejón de Jorge Juan 12*. Hip clothing for women that will place you apart from the pack from this design diva who rose to fame as the designer of the racy 1980's Movida (*see p. 118*)—for which her daring clothes provided the perfect match. Still very much at the cutting edge, though matured slightly—as have her prices. There's cheaper stuff available next door; have a look also at her younger range, Jocomomola. Always one to keep moving and not rest on her laurels, she has also started offering homeware, perhaps defying her Movida roots. *M* Retiro **Map p. 132, D1–D2**

Agatha Ruiz de la Prada *C/Marqués de Riscal*. Another exceptional dresser of the Movida whose goal it is to steer entirely clear of the trends of the international catwalks. Striking clothes for both sexes with prominent colours and ever-so-loud but stylish accessories. Has also moved into clothes for children and household items. *M* Rubén Darío **Map p. 132, B1**

Amaya Arzuaga *C/Lagasca 50*. Ever impressive innovative designs with a distinctive punky edge from this internationally and locally renowned young designer. Note her mixing of black with bright colours. The shop interior, designed by Francesc Pons, provides the perfect showcase for Arzuaga's talents. Womenswear is at street level, while the men's collection is tucked downstairs in the basement next to wines from the designer's father, plus a small bar. *M* Velázquez **Map p. 132, C2**

Ekseptión *C/Velázquez 28*. Great one-stop shop for some of the most unique clothes that Spain has to offer for both sexes, including Sybilla and Antoni Miró. Like all one-stop shops you might have to pay a bit of a premium. Step in through the striking doorway and be mesmerised. *M* Velázquez **Map p. 132, C2**

Pedro del Hierro *C/Serrano 24 & 63*. This internationally renowned designer has been beguiling women for 30 years now with hip and elegant designs that draw something from the past though never look dated. Classic designs for men too, with a colourful twist. Also does his own range of perfumes. If you miss him in town, you can catch one of his stores at the airport. *M* Serrano **Map p. 132, D2 and C2**

Purificación García *C/Serrano 28*. Very popular, mature designer clothing for men and women covering a plethora of styles for all occasions. *M* Serrano **Map p. 132, C2**

Loewe *C/Serrano 26 & 34*. Predominantly dealing in leather, though other fabrics as well, Loewe has overhauled its somewhat traditional image with the help of a team of younger, more savvy designers. Top quality clothes, shoes and accessories with prices to match. Branches are to be found all around Madrid. *M* Serrano **Map p. 132, C2**

Dickens *C/General Pardiñas 6*. Tailor-made shirts from over 300 different fabrics. *M* Príncipe de Vergara/ Velázquez **Map p. 132, C3**

FOOD

Mallorca *C/Serrano 6*. Gourmet delicatessen chain with a mouth-watering selection of sweets, cakes, the finest cold cuts, quality wines, cava, liquors, salmon and truffles. It also has a café and restaurant. For the health-conscious, Mallorca a serves a far from boring low-fat menu, stacked with proteins and minerals, put together with the help of nutrition expert Dr Marta Aranzadi. *M* Retiro **Map p. 132, D2**

Mercado de La Paz *C/Ayala 28*. Salamanca's own upmarket take on the colourful, brash and bustling neighbourhood market, with outstanding produce to match. La Boulette at stands 63–68 is a cheese lover's dream come true. *M* Serrano **Map p. 132, C2**

Mercado de Torrijos *C/General Díaz Porlier 8*. In you fancy lean meat, this is the place to come, since Torrijos specialises in beef fresh from fighting bulls. Stacked with quality Iberian produce and a wealth of species from its seas, it is a very good place to stock up. It also boasts eight types of poultry and eggs. *M* Goya/Príncipe de Vergara **Map p. 132, C4**

Jamonia *C/Ayala 142*. Upmarket *jamón* joint specialising in ham and sausages that come from pigs reared solely on acorns on the plains of Extremadura. Loads more meat besides. *M* Manuel Becerra/Lista **Map beyond p. 132, C4**

JEWELLERY

Concha García *C/Goya 38*. García has two shop-showrooms displaying striking ethnic and contemporary jewellery. Ethiopian, Tanzanian,

Togolese and Nigerian are amongst the African cultures represented. There are also Islamic jewels from the 18th–19th centuries. *M* Goya **Map p. 132, C3**

Del Pino *C/Serrano 48*. Stunning costume jewellery to top off that evening dress. *M* Serrano **Map p. 132, C2**

La Oreja de Plata *C/Jorge Juan 12*. Contemporary jewellery from Barcelona-born Chus Bures, plus a host of other items from the cheap to the outlandishly expensive. The shop itself is a gem. *M* Velázquez **Map p. 132, D3**

Helena Rohner *C/Castelló 5*. Silver chains topped off in all manner of creative ways using enamel, finest wood, precious stones, leather and so forth. Rohner believes you should sleep in your jewellery. *M* Príncipe de Vergara **Map p. 132, D3**

Barcena *Callejón de Jorge Juan 18*. Specialists in antique jewellery, with gorgeous gems dating back over a hundred years. *M* Serrano **Map p. 132, D2**

LINGERIE

Women's Secret *C/Velázquez 48*. Creative underwear at decent prices from the casual to the classy, with a similar philosophy for its accessories. Also sells swimwear, skin care products and childrens' underwear. Over 30 branches in Madrid and immediate surroundings. *M* Velázquez **Map p. 132, C3**

¡Oh, qué Luna! *C/Ayala 32*. Sizzling underwear to set the male pulses racing. Not much more to be said. The swimwear isn't bad either. *M* Serrano **Map p. 132, C2**

Oysho *C/Serrano 61*. Underwear and swimwear from this branch of Zara. *M* Rubén Darío **Map p. 132, B2**

PERFUME

Álvarez Gómez *C/Serrano 14*. Unique concoctions of fine scents based on carnations, roses and violets from this extraordinary perfumery that has been in business for over a century. A similar standard is reached in its marvellously detailed jewellery and accessories. Also a branch at C/Sevilla 2, close to Sol. *M* Serrano **Map p. 132, D2**

Barfumería *C/Conde de Aranda 4*. Basement shop for both sexes with a wide range of enticing-sounding brand names including Route du thé, Comptoir, Sud Pacifique, Comme des Garçons, Eve Lom, and Odile Lecoin. *M* Retiro/Serrano **Map p. 132, D2**

Waza *C/General Díaz Porlier 30*. Perfume with a strong sense of origin—especially those from Cologne, Provence, Syria and, naturally, Spain. The jewellery is also worth a nose around. *M* Goya/Lista **Map p. 132, C3**

SHOES

Camper *C/Ayala 13*. Perhaps the most fashionable shoes that are genuinely comfy and reasonably priced at the same time. You'll recognise their bowling-style shoes instantly: Camper is seen by some as responsible for propelling them back into style the world over a couple of years back. Branches across Madrid. *M* Serrano **Map p. 132, C2**

Farrutx *C/Serrano 7*. Minimalist layout that lets the cutting edge shoes, boots and bags do the talking. This very successful Majorcan company also deals in jackets and belts with a difference. There's another store at C/Fuencarral 67, plus several others in the city. *M* Serrano **Map p. 132, D2**

Hangar Zapatos *C/Hermosilla 70*. Eye-catching shoes for young women who want to put their best foot forward, from designers including Pedro García, Pura López, Úrsula Mascaró, Luis Onofre, and Les Tropeziennes and Blay. Another branch at C/Gaztambide 8. *M* Goya **Map p. 132, C4**

Columela *C/Columela 6*. Another of those minimalist shoe shops with über-fashionable women's shoes and accessories from designers including Juan Antonio López, Miss Rossi and Red. Sells it own brand, Mascolumela, on top. Jewellery from Raquel Moreno, Medicine Douce, Carmen Mazarrasa and Zoe Cotlenko. *M* Retiro **Map p. 132, D2**

SHOPPING CENTRES

El Jardín de Serrano *C/Goya 6–8*. Open 10am–10pm Mon–Sat. Upmarket 'boutique' shopping centre claiming to be the best and most exclusive in Madrid, with many big (and pricey) Spanish labels represented. Also houses the suitably upscale Mallorca Café in the basement, where live piano or string music accompanies the drinks, snacks and meals. *M* Serrano **Map p. 132, C2**

ABC Serrano *C/Serrano 61*. Multi-level shopping centre packed with a large range of mainly international clothing brands, cafés, restaurants and fitness centres. On the ground floor La Tienda del Tabaco is worth checking out for smokers. *M* Serrano **Map p. 132, B2**

WATCHES

The Watch Outlet *C/Jorge Juan 39*. Leading brands and traditional timepieces at discounted prices due to the shop's acquisition of watches from closing watch stores, trade fairs and the like. *M* Velázquez **Map p. 132, C3**

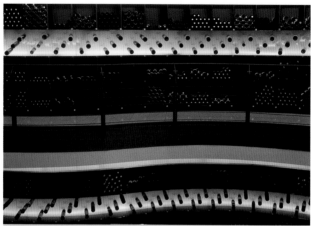

The ultra-stylish Lavinia wine-merchant

WINE

Mantequerías Bravo *C/Ayala 24*. If a good bottle of vino is what you're after, you won't go far wrong here. There's a lot to choose from, too, accompanied with cheese and *jamón* and the like. A good place for sherry as well. *M* Serrano **Map p. 132, C2**

Casa Larreina *C/Padilla 42*. More than 1,400 different wines and spirits across a broad price spectrum offering excellent quality. *M* Núñez de Balboa **Map p. 132, B3**

Lavinia *C/José Ortega y Gasset 16*. A veritable paradise for wine lovers, with wines stored in rooms of varying temperatures to suit their precious elixirs. This is where the rich and famous come to pick up their supplies. *M* Núñez de Balboa **Map p. 132, B3**

TRIPS OUT OF TOWN

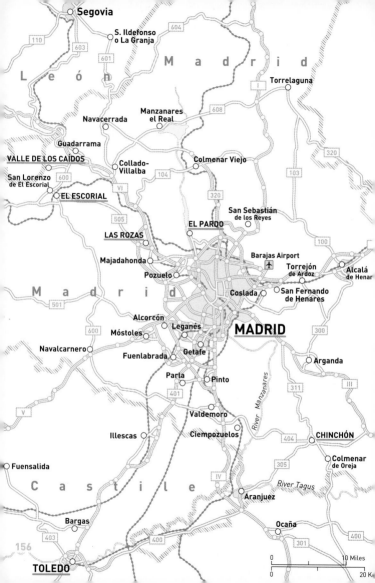

If Madrid ever gets too fast and frantic for you, the wild plains of Spain—the land of Don Quixote, windmills, medieval castles and Moorish monuments—is never far away. In fact its proximity to the old Spain makes it incredibly easy to hop on a bus or a train, and before you know it you can reach such gems as the amazingly well preserved Toledo, the centre of medieval Spain.

Thanks to the remarkable speeds clocked up by the AVE trains, Córdoba in the heart of Andalucia is reachable in under an hour and three quarters, despite lying 400 km south of the capital. Here are a few suggestions within very easy striking distance of the city.

Palacio Real del Pardo

TELEPHONE 91 376 1500
GETTING THERE Buses run regularly from Moncloa (map p. 102, B2).

Franco's main residence and workplace, located nine kilometres northwest of Madrid, was once the hunting lodge of Carlos I. The ever-popular court architect Francesco Sabatini was brought in by Carlos III to complete the palace, adding to the original lodge, while Bayeu and Maella painted some splendid murals.

The elaborate Bourbon interior contrasts with Franco's austere workrooms. Inside there's the chapel where Franco prayed, and the theatre where films were censored during the fascist regime. Next to the palace is the pavilion-like Casita del Príncipe, built by Juan de Villanueva.

Today the palace is often used to accommodate foreign heads of state, and is handy for the Palacio de la Zarzuela close by, which is home to the Spanish Royal Family.

Despite the association with the former dictator, the town and the palace make a popular day out for the citizens of Madrid, with El Pardo's smart restaurants serving game along the Avenida de la Guardia, and a handful of swanky country clubs.

Nearby there is also the **Las Rozas Village** outlet shopping centre, with last season's collections from big name brands and designers a-plenty, all reduced by up to 60%. Includes the like of Antonio Miró, Farrutx, Loewe, Women's Secret, Camper, Fun&Basics, Cristina Castañer and international names Hugo Boss, Tommy Hilfiger and Gas—to name but a few. *Buses leave every 20 minutes from Moncloa bus station (map p. 102, B2). Journey time 40 minutes. Price €1.70. Las Rozas is open Mon–Fri, Sun and bank holidays 11am–9pm, Sat 11am–10 pm. Closed Dec 25 and Jan 1st and 6th. www.LasRozasVillage.com* **Map pp. 2–3**

El Escorial and Valle de los Caídos

GETTING THERE	By bus take Herranz from Moncloa (platform 3; map p. 102, B2) for €3.20.
CHARGES	Standard entry to the El Escorial complex is €8 (€4 concession), though free to EU citizens on Wednesdays.

People tend either to love or hate this imposing and austere construction—Philip II's monumental folly that dominates the plains for miles and miles. Work began in 1563 and lasted 21 years, with responsibility for the construction passing from Juan Bautista de Toledo to Juan de Herrera on the former's death. 'Simplicity in the construction, severity in the whole; nobility without arrogance, majesty without ostentation' was their order from the king, and between them they oversaw the completion of an impressive set of building stats that would have modern day property developers frothing at the mouth. Measuring 205 by 160 metres, El Escorial has 16 courtyards, 15 cloisters, 1,200 doors and 2,600 windows. Philip II is known to have closely overseen the building. Perhaps the most striking thing about El Escorial is the sheer sight of it for the first time. While a lot of its art treasures have been relocated to the Prado (Philip II was a Bosch buff as well as a lover of Titian), there are still many works by Italian masters here, for example Tintoretto, Veronese and Luca Giordano, as well as by Spaniards Velázquez, Zurbarán, and Ribera, the Greek El Greco, not to mention Bosch. Many of the best paintings are in the chapter houses. The Basilica (to which entry is free) has 45 altars, with ceiling frescoes by Luca Cambiaso and Luca Giordano.

The town of San Lorenzo de El Escorial is a pleasant place to visit, and has some nice places to take a bite, too, especially La Cueva (*C/San Antón 4, T 91 890 1516*), which was founded in 1768.

VALLE DE LOS CAÍDOS

GETTING THERE There is one bus a day from the bus station at San Lorenzo de El Escorial leaving at 3.15pm and leaving Valle de los Caídos at 5.30pm. Tickets (€8) are available at the ticket office, not on board the bus. The fare includes entrance to the basilica.

'The valley of the fallen' is where Generalísimo Franco put Republican prisoners to work after the war, and the monuments constructed are supposedly a tribute to all those claimed by the Civil War, though in reality it was more of a Spanish gulag. Below the gigantic cross on the hill, 150 metres high and 46 metres wide, propped up by ghoulish figures, you enter an underground basilica which tunnels into the mountainside. It is quite a bizarre experience, but one not to be missed. The Fascist, almost Nazi, symbolism is striking and unsettling: two giant, muscular winged angels (eerie rather than reassuring) guard the entrance to the enormous tunnel-like chamber, a place where you'd be forgiven for expecting to run into the most unimaginable underground sect. In fact on November 21 every year, die-hard Franco supporters make the trip from Madrid to the Basilica, where Franco is interred.

Step outside back into the fresh air for sweeping views across the Sierra de Guadarrama, or better still take the funicular up to the base of the cross (for a small fee).

Chinchón

GETTING THERE A bus operated by La Veloz goes hourly from close to Madrid's Conde de Casal metro station (just beyond map p. 9, D4). Price: €3.50; journey time: 50 minutes. By car, leave the city on the A4 highway and then take the M404.

Just 45 km southeast of Madrid, attractive Chinchón offers a pleasant change of pace from the capital and serves as a haven of retreat for burnt out Madrileños. Its real attraction is its main square, with its wonky wooden balconies looking out onto the Plaza Mayor, which is still used to host bullfights and an Easter passion play. You might also recognize it from a much-screened World Cup 2002 advert. Overlooking the main square is the Iglesia de la Asunción, which is worth a look for a Goya *Assumption*.

The main square can even be packed on winter afternoons, with revellers tucking into hearty Castilian roasts or sampling the local firewater: anis, which comes in both sweet and dry varieties and is regarded as the best in Spain. You'll pass the distilleries on the way into town. There are also one or two curious yellowy-green liquors to be found tucked away behind the bars.

Higher prices are charged in the square, but literally just off it the prices drop considerably. This is truly a place for a good feed and drink. Specialities are lamb cooked in a wood-burning oven, or suckling pig—and much larger than average menus abound.

Toledo

GETTING THERE Buses take one hour to reach Toledo and leave from Madrid's Estación Sur de Autobuses (map pp. 2–3) every half hour. The bus drops off just outside the old city. Less frequent trains depart from Estación de Atocha (map p. 8, D4; journey time: 90mins), and leave you further away. By car, take the N-401 highway heading south.

The ancient city of Toledo was Spain's capital from the time when Ferdinand and Isabella united the powerful houses of Aragon and Castile and conquered the rest of the Iberian peninsula from the Moors, until Philip II, husband of England's Mary Tudor and the man behind the ill-fated Armada, moved his seat of government to Madrid. The town today is a wondrous maze of medieval charm with a stunning 13th-century Gothic cathedral and a domineering seen-it-all Alcázar. All of this and more is perched above the Río

El Greco: *Burial of the Count of Orgaz* (1586; detail)

Tajo (the Tagus), which winds it way around the ancient cocktail of Moorish, Christian and Jewish architecture.

Toledo is also home to a fabulous El Greco masterpiece: the *Entierro del Conde de Orgaz* ('Burial of the Count of Orgaz'), housed in the Mudéjar-towered church of Santo Tomé on the Plaza del Conde. The count is depicted receiving a dramatic send-off by his Toledan contemporaries (which include El Greco himself, fifth to the right of the hooded friar) as the angelic and deceased—all trademark and defining El Greco figures—await him and welcome him to the heavens. The count is actually buried directly below the painting, and Toledo, which is where El Greco lived when he settled permanently in Spain, still has a number of his paintings.

Toledo's close proximity to the capital means that it is often swamped with day-trippers, so it's worth staying over to better appreciate the city's charm—especially if you're around during Holy Week, when the slightly sinister Easter processions of *Semana Santa*, with hooded penitents pulling floats laden with divine images, throng the city streets.

eating and drinking

TAPAS

Tapas have become a global phenomenon, and are a way of eating that transcends linguistic barriers. Not that the dishes don't have established names, but many tapas bars have their offerings laid out on the bar, so you can dispense with a menu and get what you want by pointing. The variety of tapas served is vast, and this provides an ideal way of getting acquainted with the country's varied cuisine. Tapas bars tend to be concentrated in bunches, so it's easy to skip from bar to bar, nibbling a bit of whatever takes the fancy. In recent years as tapas have taken on the world, the home of tapas is busy reinventing itself with some new, more sophisticated delicacies—especially in the tapas havens of Madrid's La Latina district. But lovers of tradition have no cause for panic: Madrid still has plenty of places where the old standards abound.

Tapas originated as a wedge of bread or ham placed on top of a glass of wine (tapa means 'lid'). Now the term covers anything and everything from bread and olives to baby octopus and sea slugs. In many bars you'll be given a little titbit of tapas along with your drink. And however puny such measures may be—it could be as little as a couple of crisps—it is still undeniably warming the way these snacks are placed in front of you as you settle into your drink.

It also quite normal, barring perhaps the swishest bar in the upmarket Salamanca district, to cast the remnants of your snack onto the floor at your feet, and it's definitely something of a *faux pas* to stuff discarded prawn heads, olive stones, etc. into the ashtray or to put them back on the plate. Do as the Madrileños do and chuck it on the floor—they consider it more hygienic this way, and the floors are regularly swept. Spanish bars certainly bring a new meaning to the phrase spit and sawdust!

In Madrid's bars, throwing your rubbish on the floor is absolutely normal

Devouring tapas can mean anything from ordering a *ración*, a larger portion than a *tapa*, and good for sharing, or perhaps a canapé, which is something on a small piece of bread. In the Basque tradition, where these are laid out temptingly on the counter-top, they are known as *pinchos*. Also common in tapas bars are *bocadillos* and *bocatas*, essentially sandwiches made from a bread roll or baguette. What goes between the bread, whether it be tangy manchego cheese, *jamón*, *tortilla*, baby squid or anchovies, is sure to please. It's usually a bit cheaper to eat at the bar than sit down to the chow at a table.

Spain wouldn't be Spain without chunky legs of cured ham hanging from the ceiling. The country is the world's biggest producer of ham—roughly one for each and every Spaniard each year. Not all that much of it is exported, either, for Spain is also the largest consumer of the stuff. Jamón Serrano is the standard cured ham. It tastes like it does through the simple effects of salt, air and time. Jamón Ibérico is the gourmet version, made from pigs grazed on acorns that impart a more smokey and refined flavour.

SOME TYPICAL TAPAS

Aceitunas – olives
Ahumados – smoked fish—anything from trout to seafish
Anchoas – anchovies
Berberechos – cockles
Boquerones – white anchovies in vinegar
Calamares a la romana – deep fried squid rings
Chopito – baby octopus
Chorizo – spicy sausage
Croquetas – filled croquettes
Gambas – prawns
Patatas bravas – fried potatoes in a spicy sauce
Tortilla española – Spanish omelette (made with potatoes)

THE MENÚ DEL DÍA

Whether these great value daily menus where initially spawned from the need to satisfy hungry workers or even leisured visitors in need of a good feed, the three-course set lunches, which offer several choices for each course, offered in so many places across town, are quite often outstanding value for money. They start from as little as seven euros a head and include bread and anything from a glass to a flask of wine, or even a bottle in some generous establishments.

Menús del día abound in restaurants across Madrid, and it can often be a good way of trying out one of the more expensive restaurants, who charge high prices for à la carte, but still offer a budget *menú* at lunchtime. Despite the increasing pressures of the modern global business world—of which Madrid is very much a part—a good, long, leisurely lunch is still a pretty serious phenomenon here. It's anything but uncommon to find yourself

queuing up in some of the better places, and this can lead to quite
a panic as it gets to the end of the lunch hour, or rather hours!
Evening menus, the *menú de la noche*, are also quite common.

THE GASTRONOMIC SPANISH PARADISE

From the haute cuisine of the Basque country to the roasts of
Castile, Valencian paella, the fried fish of Andalucia, chicken
roasted in cider from the Asturias and the seafood of Galicia, you
can find it all in the capital. Menus are forever changing too, as the
taste for experiment grows, and chefs strive to infuse more variety
into their cooking. The tendency is starting to transform the once-
standard daily offerings. Nevertheless, the old Madrid staple of
cocido a la madrileña—a stew made up of chicken, beef, more
meats, chickpeas and veggies—is worth a dabble once in a while.

Despite being stuck right in the middle of the Iberian peninsula,
hundreds of kilometres from the sea and just about as landlocked
as you can get in Spain, Madrid boasts wonderful seafood
(*marisco*). Tonnes of it is plucked fresh from the sea every day, and
along with many varieties of saltwater fish, it arrives in the city by
the trainload before being shunted with speed to restaurants.

WINE

When leading wine critic Robert Parker recently heralded Spain
as the future king of world wines, he might have shaken up a few
big guns from Spain's colossal wine-making northern neighbour,
France. The truth is, though, that many of those familiar with the
rapidly rising standards already knew it. Spain's wines are truly
coming to fruition as the new generation of winemakers is
experimenting, leveraging the benefits of new technology with
some of the best vineyards known to man.

Spain's vintners are concentrating much more on quality rather
than the quantity that fixated them for so long, and the
cooperative approach to winemaking—an inheritance of Franco—
is no longer the norm.

The classic and world-renowned red wine-making regions of

Rioja and Ribera del Duero are now being rivalled by a host of young pretenders, yielding ever more engaging wine. Look out for upcoming reds from regions like Toro, Jumilla and Priorat, all quite distinct from each other, and indeed from anything else in the wine-making world. The long-discarded indigenous white Albariño grape, that hails from Rías Baixas on the northwest coast in Galicia, is a classic example of old world charm made with new world refinement, and its wines are aromatic and feisty. The region of Rueda is renowned for soft fruity whites.

And while technology and terroir count for a lot, the raw material is important too, and here the Spanish difference can be truly felt. While the rest of the world plants Cabernet Sauvignon and Chardonnay, Spain is capitalising on its indigenous varieties, turning soft and fruity Garnacha (well, not entirely indigenous, as the French have a claim on it too, known north of the Pyrenees as Grenache) and light, spicy Tempranillo into some of the world's most drinkable and affordable wine.

Added to this are a smattering of international varieties, notably Cabernet Sauvignon and Syrah. Some of these grapes also really hit it off with their Spanish cousins, and make for some unique and smooth blends.

For sparkling wine, the cavas of Catalonia have a deserved reputation, and at a snip of the price of champagne they are generally fine value for money.

The sun-drenched, dark treacle-like sherries of Andalucia, from the likes of Pedro Jiménez, provide a wonderful accompaniment to dessert, while the dry finos are ideal for kicking the taste buds into action as an aperitif.

And while on the subject of vino, we must not forget the old fortified wine-derivative *vermut*, which flows freely in Madrid, especially at weekends before lunch.

You can often happen upon rare gems in the unlikeliest of bars, though it must be said there's still a lot of rough stuff flowing around. Wine that meets all the appellation requirements carries a Denominación de Origen (D.O) stamp.

BEER AND SPIRITS

Beer (*cerveza*) is just as popular as wine, and for the most thirst-quenching opt for the golden *nectar de barril* (draft). Typical measures include the small *caña*, the mid-sized *tubo* and the *jarra*, which approaches pint-size.

The usual international spirits abound, with some local takes on established poisons, such as Larios Gin. Pacharán, the colour of sloe gin, is a liquor/spirit that hails from Navarra and is made from the pacharán berry.

Café in Plaza Mayor

COFFEE

Madrileños drink plenty of coffee—not surprising really, when you consider their furious-paced lifestyle. Spain is also one one country where Italian styles of coffee have not proliferated. The Spanish still take their coffee in the Spanish way. The main ways to order coffee are given below.

Cafe solo: Black espresso

Cafe cortado: Literally espresso 'cut' with a dash of milk. If you prefer a milkier version, ask for it *'corto de café'*.

Cafe con leche: Coffee with a generous measure of milk, usually hot, sometimes cold. For a larger measure ask for a *taza grande*.

Cafe americano: Made the same way as espresso, but with much more water, giving a lighter-flavoured and more substantial cup.

Cafe con hielo: Coffee with ice. The ice and coffee are supplied separately so that you can dissolve your sugar in the coffee before pouring it over the ice cubes.

Carajillo: Coffee animated with a measure or two of a spirit, such as brandy, rum, or anis. It can serve as quite a 'pick me up' on a long night out, and induce that second or third wind.

Cappuccino: Though this is served in more upmarket places, it is manifestly un-Spanish, and hardly craved, given the excellent native coffee that abounds.

entertainment

INFORMATION
TICKETS
CINEMA
THEATRE, OPERA & DANCE
MUSIC

INFORMATION

Spanish daily papers *El País* and *El Mundo* run daily listings, and on Fridays both publish comprehensive sections devoted to events, bars and restaurants in the capital. The *Guía del Ocio* (www.guiadelocio.com) comes out every Friday and covers cinema, theatre, concerts, exhibitions, restaurants and nightlife. The Madrid Tourist Board also distributes the free and bi-lingual *Qué hacer—what's on in Madrid*, which it publishes monthly.

TICKETS

As well as from all the box offices of the venue themselves a number of establishments sell tickets:

El Corte Inglés Tickets available in all Madrid branches. www.elcorteingles.es

Madrid Rock (for rock concerts) *Gran Vía 25, T 91 523 2652. Open 10.30am–3.15pm and 4.30pm–9pm.* **M** Gran Vía. **Map p. 8, A1**

FNAC *C/Preciados 28, T 91 595 6200. Open 10am–9.30pm, every day except Sun when it opens at noon.* **M** Callao. **Map p. 8, A1**

CINEMA

A number of cinemas show films in their original version (V.O.), listings for which can be found in most major newspapers. The main ones are:

Alphaville *C/Martín de los Heros 12, T 91 559 3836.* **M** Plaza de España. **Map p. 102, D3**

California *C/Andrés Mellado 53, T 91 5440058. M* Moncloa. **Map p. 102, B3**

Filmoteca Nacional *C/Santa Isabel 3, T 91 369 1125. M* Antón Martín. **Map p. 8, C2**

Ideal Multicines *C/Doctor Cortezo 6, T 91 369 2518. M* Tirso de Molina. **Map p. 8, C1**

Luna *C/Luna 2, T 91 522 4752. M* Callao. **Map p. 68, A4**

Princesa *C/Princesa 3, T 91 541 4100. M* Plaza de España. **Map p. 102, D4**

Renoir (next door to Alphaville) *C/Martín de los Heros 14, T 91 541 4100. M* Plaza de España. **Map p. 102, D3**

Renoir Cuatro Caminos *C/Raimundo Fernández Villaverde 10, T 91 541 4100. M* Cuatro Caminos

Renoir Retiro *C/Narvaez 42, T 91 541 4100. M* Ibiza. **Map p. 9, A3**
Rosales *C/Quintana 22, T 91 541 5800. M* Argüelles. **Map p. 102, C3**

THEATRE, OPERA & DANCE

The Centro Dramático Nacional is housed at the Teatro María Guerrero (*C/Tamayo y Baus 4, T 91 319 4769, Map p. 132, D1*) and hosts top-rate productions of Spanish and international plays. It also puts on plays at the Sala Olímpia at Plaza Lavapiés (*T 91 527 4622, Map p. 8, C2*). The acclaimed Adolfo Marsillach directs the Compañia Nacional de Teatro Clásico, which delivers the classics from legendary playwrights Lope de Vega and Tirso de Molina

CLASSICAL MUSIC

The principal concert venue is the Auditorio Nacional de Música (just above the Museo de la Ciudad). *C/Príncipe de Vergara 146, T 91 337 0100. M* Cruz del Rayo/Concha Espina. **Map pp. 2–3**

planning

TOURIST OFFICES
GETTING AROUND
EMERGENCIES & MEDICAL
EMBASSIES
OPENING HOURS
PUBLIC HOLIDAYS
SIGHTSEEING TOURS
PLACES TO STAY

TOURIST OFFICES

The Spanish National Tourist Office provides an extensive range of brochures, leaflets and festivals.

IN THE UK

Spanish National Tourist Office 22-23 Manchester Square, London W1U 3PX. T: (Information) 020 7486 8077 T: (24-hour Brochure Request Line) 09063 640 630 (calls cost 60 pence per minute); Fax: 020 7486 8034 www.uk.tourspain.es; londres@tourspain.es

IN THE US AND CANADA

New York: Tourist Office of Spain, 666 5th Avenue, 35th floor, New York NY 10103 T: 1 212 265 8822, Fax: 1 212 265 8864, www.okspain.org

Los Angeles: Tourist Office of Spain, 8383 Wilshire Boulevard, Suite 956, Beverly Hills, CA 90211 T: 1 323 658 7188, Fax: 1 323 658 1061, losangeles@tourspain.es

Chicago: Tourist Office of Spain, Water Tower Place, Suite 915 East, 845 North Michigan Avenue, Chicago, Ill 60611, T: 1 312 642 1992, Fax: 1 312 642 9817, chicago@tourspain.es

Miami: Tourist Office of Spain, 1221 Brickell Avenue, Siute 1850 Florida 33131. T: 1 305 358 1992, Fax: 1 305 358 8223, oetmiami@tourspain.es

Canada: Tourist Office of Spain, 2 Bloor St. West, Suite 3402, Toronto, Ontario, M4W 3E2, T: 1 416 961 3131, Fax: 1 416 961 1992, www.tourspain.toronto.on.ca, toronto@tourspain.es

IN MADRID

The regional government of Madrid runs a very useful tourist office at C/Duque de Medinaceli 2, T 91 429 4951. **Map p. 8, B3**

The City Council runs the Oficina Municipal de Información Turística in the heart of the tourist city at Plaza Mayor 3, T 91 366 5477. Open 10 am–8pm Mon–Fri, 10 am–2 pm Sat, Sun and holidays. **Map p. 68, B4**. It also operates the Patronato Municipal de Turismo at C/Mayor 69, T 91 588 2900, Open 8am–3pm and 4pm–6pm Mon to Thur, and 8am–3pm on Fri. **Map p. 68, B4**

GETTING TO THE CITY CENTRE FROM THE AIRPORT

A taxi should not cost much more than €15: €20 is the absolute maximum. It is quite common for foreigners to be fleeced: to avoid this, ignore the taxi drivers who might approach you in the arrivals lounge and head for the taxi rank outside. Make sure the meter's running.

Barajas Airport is now connected to the metro system and the journey can be done on a single ticket that costs just €1.15, less if you buy 10 rides, *abono de diez viajes*, for €5.80, which is also good for buses. However, getting to the centre involves at least a couple of changes, though you whip through to Nuevos Minsterios in the business district in just 12 minutes.

Buses run every 10 minutes to Plaza de Colón and take between 20 and 40 minutes depending on the traffic. There you can get onto the metro system, take buses or a taxi.

GETTING AROUND

Madrid has a wonderfully modern and efficient transport system, though the centre of Madrid is quite compact and walking around is a great way to get a feel for the city's different *barrios*. The metro runs from 6am to 2am, while buses run from 6am to midnight, being replaced by a fairly comprehensive network of night buses.

EMERGENCIES

National Police T 091

Ambulance Cruz Roja (Red Cross) T 91 522 2222

Fire Brigade T 080

MEDICAL SERVICES

Treatment is provided free to EU citizens with an E111 form at the Accident & Emergency (Urgencias) department of state hospitals:

Hospital General Gregorio Marañón, C/Doctor Esquerdo 46, T 91 586 8000

Hospital Clínico San Carlos, Plaza de Cristo Rey, T 91 549 7433/330 3758

Ciudad Sanitaria La Paz, Paseo de la Castellana 261, T 91 734 2600

The Unidad Médica Angloamericana, C/Conde de Aranda 1, T 91 435 1823, is a private clinic with English-speaking doctors and dentists.

LATE-NIGHT CHEMISTS

Madrid runs a rota system for late-night and weekend opening, which is displayed in pharmacy windows and listed in newspapers, such as *El País*, or is available on T 010. At least one is open in each district of the city, though be prepared to knock for assistance. 24/7 chemists include:

Farmacia del Globo, Plaza de Antón Martín 46, *M* Antón Martín

Real Farmacia de la Reina Madre C/Major 59, *M* Ópera

Farmacia Velázquez 70, C/Velázquez 70, *M* Velázquez

LOST OR STOLEN PROPERTY

The process or reporting a theft is known as a *denuncia* and is a necessary step in claiming insurance.

Credit Card Companies:

Visa: T 900 999 124

Mastercard: T 900 971 231

American Express: T 915 720 303 or T 902 375 637

Diners Club: T 915 474 000

EMBASSIES

American Embassy: C/Serrano 75, T 91 587 2200

Australian Embassy: Plaza del Descrubridor Diego de Ordás 3, T 91 441 9300

British Embassy: C/Fernando del Santo 16, T 91 308 0618

British Consulate: C/Marqués de la Ensenada 16, T 91 308 5201

Canadian Embassy: C/Núñez de Balboa 35, T 91 431 4300

Irish Embassy: Paseo de la Castellana 46, T 91 576 3500

New Zealand Embassy: Plaza de la Lealtad, 2 T 91 523 0226

OPENING HOURS

Smaller shops tend to close at lunchtime and on Saturday afternoons. Many larger shops, department stores and shopping centres stay open all day.

Banks open Mon–Fri 8.30 am–2 pm, with main branches staying open until 4/5 pm. Most banks are open on Sat 8.30 am–12/1 pm.

PUBLIC HOLIDAYS

1 January – New Year's Day

6 January – Epiphany

Easter Thursday and Easter Friday

May 1 – Labour Day

May 2 – Madrid Day

May 15 – San Isidro (in 2005 moved to September 9th)

July 25th – Santiago Apostol (Patron Saint of Spain, Madrid Community only)

August 15 – Assumption of the BVM

October 12 – Spanish National Day

November 1 – All Saints' Day

December 6 – Constitution Day

December 8 – Immaculate Conception

December 25 – Christmas Day

SIGHTSEEING TOURS

Madrid Vision Tourist bus with 1- or 2-day hop-on hop-off ticket with three routes in open-topped buses around the city, passing all major points of interest. Discount at all the major sights. Tickets available on the buses or at tourist offices. €13 and €17 for adults, €7 and €9 for 7 to 16 year-olds for one- and two-day passes respectively. Under 7s free.

The **Madrid Card** costs €39, €58 and €76 for 1, 2 and 3 days respectively and gives free admission to 40 of the main museums, unlimited use of the hop-on-hop-off tourist Madrid Vision Bus, a guided walking tour through Old Madrid on Saturdays, as well as considerable discounts in shops, restaurants, shows and leisure centres for adults and children.

PLACES TO STAY

As capital cities go, Madrid has way more than its fair share of accommodation to suit all pockets. Despite having plenty of accommodation in every price category, it still pays to book ahead as the number of short-stay trippers soars, as well as to avoid dragging your luggage around the bustling streets. Note that places fill up quickly for Madrid's top fiestas, those of Madrid's patron saint San Isidro, in May.

At the lower end there are plenty of great value *pensiones*, sometimes for as little as €20 a night, though it must be said that Madrid is also home to plenty of fleapits. The densest concentration of accommodation can be found around Puerta del Sol, Plaza de Santa Ana and the neighbourhoods of Malasaña and Chueca (for *pensiones* and *hostales*), and hotels along the Gran Vía.

Breakfast is often not included, though it is more advisable to use breakfast as a chance to sample the excellent cafés of Madrid—for which you won't have to look very far.

PASEO DEL ARTE

€€€ Hotel Ritz *Plaza de la Lealtad 5, T 91 521 2857*. Alfonso XIII's desire to improve the face of his capital was made all the more keen when he struggled to put up guests for his wedding, hampered by the lack of plush lodgings. This led to the building of a luxury hotel to rival the Ritz in Paris, with architect Charles Mewes creating a timeless classic. It stands on the edge of Retiro Park and is very handy for the Prado. With just 167 rooms, the emphasis is on old-world comfort. If you don't opt to stay here, for whatever reason, it's certainly worth dropping in for a spot of breakfast, lunch or even just a cocktail. While the atmosphere is distinctly of a bygone age, all rooms are kitted out with modern needs, like internet hookup. *M* Banco de España **Map p. 8, B4**

The Westin Palace *Plaza de las Cortes 7, T 91 360 8000*. Strikingly situated on the Plaza, centrally located and commissioned specially by Alfonso XIII in 1912. Its grand exterior gives way to an exquisite dome-covered reception. From there it's palatial comfort all the way. A stone's throw from the big three art museums and the blazing nightlife of Santa Ana. *M* Banco de España/Sevilla **Map p. 8, B3**

Hotel Villa Real *Plaza de las Cortes 10, T 91 420 2547*. A fine and tastefully decorated alternative to the Ritz and Palace, the Villa

Real knows it can't beat the other two for old world elegance, but it successfully blends the best of the old with the modern. It does this literally in each room. A fine place for art lovers, with paintings by Barcelona's finest—Antoni Tàpies—adorning the restaurant. Villa Real also has the largest private collection of ancient Roman mosaics in all Europe. *M* Banco de España **Map p. 8, B3**

Hotel Lope de Vega *C/Lope de Vega 49, T 91 360 0011*. Four-star hotel dedicated to Spain's greatest playwright, with themed rooms on the life and times of Lope de Vega himself, as well as other cultural and historical happenings of the 17th century. Rooms are decked out in cosy warm colours and have private terraces. *M* Antón Martín **Map p. 8, B3**

€€ **Hotel Santander** *C/Echegaray 1, T 91 429 6644*. Oozing old-world character and charm—and though from the outside it looks as though the rooms might be cramped, they are in fact good and spacious. The Santander also boasts an ideal central location. Step outside and on your right is a street lined with restaurants offering dishes from all around Spain and other parts of the Spanish-speaking world—though be warned: rooms on the Carrera de San Jerónimo can be noisy. *M* Sevilla/Sol **Map p. 8, B2**

Hotel El Prado *C/Prado 11, T 91 369 0234*. Very well located wine-themed three-star hotel with rooms named after Spanish wine regions. Smart and modern with internet access, private parking and a wine library. From €160 for a double. *M* Antón Martín **Map p. 8, B2**

Hotel Asturias *C/Sevilla 2, T 91 4296676*. Good value two-star very close to Sol, right in the heart of things with a charming old-world feel and welcome. Beautiful old building overlooking the Plaza Canalejas with rooms from €67 per night. *M* Sevilla **Map p. 8, B2**

Hotel Mora *Paseo del Prado 32, T 91 420 0564*. No-nonsense hotel with all the usual amenities at a good price. Opposite the Prado, though ideal for all of the Big Three. Some rooms look out on to the Paseo del Prado. The entrance is much more plush than the rooms themselves. *M* Atocha **Map p. 8, B4**

Hotel Mediodía *Plaza Emperador Carlos V 8, T 91 527 3060*. Ideal for arriving and departing by train to Atocha and a stone's throw from the Reina Sofía, this large two-star hotel of 173 rooms is comfortably kitted out and has attractive chandeliered and pillared dining and seating areas. *M* Atocha **Map p. 8, C4**

€   **Hostal Buelta** *C/Doctor Drumén 4, T 91 539 9807.* Good budget option right close by Reina Sofía. En-suite rooms with TV at €26 a single and €40 a double. *M* Atocha **Map p. 8, C4**

OLD MADRID

€€ **Hotel High Tech Clíper** *C/Chinchilla 6 (corner of Gran Vía), T 91 531 1700.* Super-modern and tastefully decorated three-star, ideal for those who need to be online whilst in Madrid. Modem-based internet connection in all rooms with free broadband ADSL in the business centre. Computers are thrown in with the highest-end rooms, as is high speed broadband. For other high-tech options in the capital from the same chain, check out www.hthoteles.com. *M* Santo Domingo **Map p. 68, B4**

€   **Hostal La Macarena** *Cava de San Miguel 8, T 91 365 9221.* Atmospherically located on a cobbled street by the Plaza Mayor, the impressive 19th-century doorway gives way to a *hostal* of considerable charm with spotless bijou rooms with en-suite pint-sized bathrooms, ceiling fans and cable TV. Helpful staff. *M* Ópera **Map p. 68, B3**

GRAN VÍA, CHUECA

€€€ **Hotel Emperador** *Gran Vía 53, T 91 547 2800.* Though not the most impressive four-star hotel in Madrid, the Emperador does boast a superb rooftop swimming pool and sunbathing terrace affording terrific views of the city. Popular place to stay with a lively bar. *M* Gran Vía **Map p. 103, D1**

€€ **Casón del Tormes** *C/Río 7, T 91 541 9746.* Peaceful and very comfortable hotel near the Plaza de las Cortes, not far from the Royal Palace. En-suite rooms with air conditioning and funky wooden headboards. A good hotel if you have a car with you as nearby there's a public car park—or for €14 per night motorists can use the hotel car park. Double rooms from €99. *M* Plaza de España **Map p. 102, D4**

€   **Hotel Mónaco** *C/Barbieri 5, T 91 522 4630.* One-star hotel perfect for staggering home from the nightlife of Chueca. Appropriately (perhaps), the building was once a brothel. Some rooms are elegantly run down, decked out in early 20th-century Art Deco and kitsch. *M* Chueca/Gran Vía **Map p. 103, D3**

SALAMANCA & RECOLETOS

€€€ Villa Magna Park Hyatt *Paseo de la Castellana 22, T 91 576 7500*. Absolutely nothing special to look at from the outside, the Villa Magna transforms to the height of luxury on the inside, and as such is the choice of many of the rich and famous. Some rooms adapted for guests with disabilities. *M* Colón/Rubén Darío **Map p. 132, B2**

Hotel Wellington *C/Velázquez 8, T 91 575 4400*. Steeped in the atmosphere of yesteryear, this slightly faded hotel lies opposite the Retiro. From €300 for a double, it's slightly cheaper than other five stars. The esteemed Goizeko Wellington restaurant next door is a major pulling point. Popular with bullfighters, it also has a Flamenco club in the basement, as well as the Bar Inglés, an attractive terrace garden with a swimming pool. *M* Retiro **Map p. 132, D2**

Hotel Santo Mauro *C/Zurbano 36, T 91 319 6900*. Luxurious 19th-century palace and former embassy with 36 individually designed rooms. Contemporary décor though retaining the original architecture and features. *M* Rubén Darío **Map p. 132, B1**

Hotel Bauza *C/Goya 79, T 91 435 7545*. Minimalist, almost designer, four-star hotel that fits in well with the neighbourhood. The same approach goes for the restaurant. *M* Goya **Map p. 132, C4**

Hotel Adler *C/Velázquez 33, T 91 426 3220*. Sophisticated boutique hotel, perfectly adapted to its location in the heart of the city's most prestigious shopping district. Modern facilities, sublime comfort and Neoclassical style in this former 19th-century bank. *M* Velázquez **Map p. 132, C2–C3**

Nh Sanvy Hotel *C/ Goya 3, T 91 756 0800*. Tastefully refurbished modern hotel on the Plaza de Colón beside the Paseo de la Castellana. Serves a plush buffet breakfast and houses a quality restaurant that specialises in Basque-Navarran cuisine. Its swimming pool is a significant draw in summer. *M* Colón **Map p. 132, C1**

art glossary

Abstract Expressionism Mid-20th-century American art movement focused on expressing powerful emotion and energy through the artistic medium (the paint), and often by the sheer size of the work.

ARCO International contemporary arts fair which takes place in Madrid in early spring.

Arroyo, Eduardo (b. 1937). Spanish artist who made his name with a series of works on world dictators, presented at the Venice Biennale in the early 60s, and which produced official howls of outrage in Franco's Spain. Works on a similar theme in the early 70s resulted in his expulsion from the country. His style is a blend of influences from Pop Art and Surrealism.

Baroque Style of art that dominated the 17th century, and which is closely associated with the Counter Reformation. The ethos of the Baroque is sensual, theatrical and dramatic, seeking to create an emotional rather than intellectual response in the viewer.

Bayeu, Francisco (1734–95) A successful career artist and competent portrait painter. Though he was director of both the Academia de San Fernando and of the Real Fábrica de Tapices (for which he produced cartoons), as well as court painter to Carlos IV, Bayeu is credited with helping the fledgling Goya (his brother-in-law) find his way to the top, and today lives forever in Goya's shadow.

Bellver, Fernando (b. 1954). Madrid-born artist whose work owes a debt to Pop Art, playing as it does on associations with familiar brands and images, and displaying a distinctive, quirky humour.

Bellver, Ricardo (1845–1924) Madrid-born sculptor, very popular in his own lifetime, whose most famous creation is the Monumento al Ángel Caído.

Bosch, Hieronymus (c. 1450–1516) Netherlandish painter whose appeal lies chiefly in the bizarre and often grotesque fantasy world which he depicts (and which the Surrealists drew on heavily). He was highly acclaimed in his own lifetime, and his works were much appreciated by Philip II of Spain, who had a fine collection of them (most now in the Prado).

Braque, Georges (1882–1963) Cubist initiator who stunned the art world with a series of landscapes of the southern French town of L'Estaque in 1908—the paintings seemingly made up of cubes. He lived very much in Picasso's shadow, spending up to a decade on a single painting, though was fervently pursued—and looked up to—by Picasso.

Brueghel family Pieter Brueghel the Elder's (c. 1525–69) connection to Spain comes through the half-sister of Philip II, who was governor of the Habsburg Netherlands. His early style was influenced by Bosch; in the last years of his life he produced the great works for which he is now chiefly known. His output includes crowded peasant scenes, notable for their skilful composition; sweeping landscapes and intimate religious pieces. His son, Jan Brueghel (1568–1625), was a gifted painter of still lifes, earning the epithet 'Velvet' for his genius at reproducing texture. He collaborated successfully with his friend and compatriot Rubens: Rubens would supply the figures, while Brueghel painted in the backgrounds.

Cano, Alonso (1601–67) Granada-born painter, sculptor and architect, known as the Spanish Michelangelo for the diversity of his talents. He worked for a time restoring the royal art collection in Madrid. His paintings, nearly all religious, are noted for their softness and sensitivity.

COBRA Short-lived (1948–51) but influential group of Expressionist artists, hailing from Denmark and the Netherlands (the name is an acronym of COpenhagen, BRussels and Amsterdam) who set themselves the task of the artistic exploration of the unconscious. A bizarre iconography of dreamlike symbols became their hallmark.

Coello, Alonso Sánchez (1531–88) Renaissance artist trained in Flanders, who became the favourite portrait painter of Philip II.

Coello, Claudio (1642–93) An important Madrid artist who became court painter in 1686. A hard worker (he studied all the Titians in the Spanish royal collection and earnestly tried to learn from them) and conscientious painter, Coello never quite received the glorious reputation he hoped for.

Cubism Probably the single most important art movement of modern times, in that it abandoned the idea that art had to imitate nature, which had been the main tenet since the Renaissance. The movement originated with Picasso and Braque. What was revolutionary about it was the way it ignored traditional ideas of perspective, and carved 3D forms up into separate planes, viewed from different angles, incorporating each into the image.

Dada Essentially a negative art movement, in that it was a response to the crisis in society caused by the First World War, and rejected everything that was established and traditional in terms of values and aesthetics. Anarchic, illogical and absurd, its greatest practitioners were Man Ray, Marcel Duchamp and Jean Arp.

Dalí, Salvador (1904–89). 'I am not a Surrealist artist,' Dalí once said, 'I am Surrealism.' This sums up not only his own attitude to himself and his genius for self-publicity, but also the place he now occupies in people's minds, as the symbol of the Surrealist movement, despite the fact that his enthusiasm for Franco led to his expulsion from the movement in 1939. His early works in fact owed a lot to Cubism, and his later works are highly Realist, and often religious. Consummate showman as well as artist, Dalí is one of the household names of the 20th century.

Dau al Set Avant-garde group founded in Barcelona shortly after the Second World War, and dedicated to a revival of Surrealism in literature and the arts, and with a predominantly Marxist ideology. Antoni Tàpies was a founder-member.

El Paso Group Heterogeneous group of artists who came together after the Second World War with the aim of reasserting Spanish artistic creativity. Their manifesto was published in 1957. The group includes artists working in a variety of styles, roughly classifiable as *art informel*. Prominent members are Rafael Canogar and Antonio Saura.

Equipo 57 Founded in 1957, 'Team 57' was a group of artists who set out to banish subjectivity, individualism and emotion and to focus on work as a collective. It disbanded in 1962.

Estudio BOPBAA Successful architecture studio founded in Barcelona in 1990 by Josep Bohigas, Francesc Pla and Iñaki Baquero.

Expressionism Artistic movement which developed in Germany in the late 19th century. It is characterised by an intensity—often violence—of expression, and by the use of unnaturalistic colours. Vincent van Gogh and Oscar Kokoschka, though vastly different in temperament, are both important Expressionist artists.

Fauvism Early 20th-century art movement characterised by the use of bold, non-naturalistic colours. The most famous *fauve* was Henri Matisse. The Expressionists later drew on Fauvist ideas.

Fernández, Gregorio (1576–1636) Sculptor and renowned exponent of the Spanish Baroque. His patrons included princes, primates and artisans' guilds, for whom he sculpted mainly altarpieces and processional figures.

Figurative art Art which depicts recognisable forms and objects, as opposed to Abstract art, which does not.

Genre painting Term used to describe a painting which depicts a scene from everyday life.

Giordano, Luca (1634–1705) Neapolitan painter of mythological and devotional subjects much admired by King Carlos II, who summoned him to Madrid, where he remained for a decade, working both there and at the Escorial.

Gómez de Mora , Juan (1586–1648) One of the great Madrid architects of the 17th century, whose harmonious works are inspired by the proportion and symmetry of the Italian Renaissance, though always betraying his love of decorative motifs. His greatest monuments are Plaza Mayor and the convent of the Encarnación.

Gordillo, Luis (b. 1934) Contemporary artist hailed as the founder of the school of 'Madrid Figurativists'. His early works were characterised by an intense use of colour; later works are sombre and more monochrome.

Goya, Francisco de (1746–1828) Helped by his brother-in-law and teacher Bayeu, Goya's first work in Madrid was as a designer in the royal tapestry factory (his designs are in the Prado). His career as an artist took off after 1780, when he became a member of the Real Academia de San Fernando. Shortly afterwards he was appointed painter to the royal household, and his warts-and-all portraits of the Spanish royal family (now in the Prado) are famous for their refusal to flatter their subjects. Illness left Goya completely deaf after 1793, at which point his work takes on a more disturbing character: the bizarre, nightmarish and slightly creepy nature of his mature works make an indelible impression. Goya also painted a number of controversial works: outspoken criticisms of the horrors of war (eg: *The Executions on Príncipe Pío Hill*, Prado) and erotic pieces (*Nude Maja*, Prado) for which he was called before the Inquisition.

Greco, El (1541–1614) Though he was born in Crete, Domenicos Theotocopoulos settled in Spain (chiefly in Tóledo) and became the first truly great exponent of the Spanish School. He is celebrated chiefly for his portraits, or for paintings were the human figure is the primary focus. Instantly recognizable are the elongated lineaments and the vivid palette.

Gris, Juan (1887–1927) Born within a stone's throw of Sol, Gris was much more than a follower in the wake of Picasso and Braque's Cubism movement: his separated forms are very much his own and instantly identifiable. The Reina Sofía has an extensive collection of his works, the Thyssen has *El Fumador* ('The Smoker'), while Spanish telecom company Telefónica has a good collection which it exhibits on a temporary basis.

Group Zero (Zero) Named after the countdown for a rocket launch: the name was intended to usher in a new beginning free of the constraints of the past: in this case one step on from Art Informel, i.e. art without form. Zero was formed in Düsseldorf in 1957 by Otto Piene and Heinz Mack. Joined by Günther Uecker, Yves Klein, Piero Manzoni, Jean Tinguely and Lucio Fontana, the movement focused on using light and movement to lift works off the canvas, ending up somewhere between painting and sculpture.

Gutiérrez Solana, José (1886–1945) Realist painter of multi-figure scenes of late19th-century Madrid. His most famous work is his *Tertulia in the Café Pombo* (Reina Sofía).

Herrera, Juan de (c. 1530–97) Architect and loyal servant of two Spanish monarchs, the Emperor Charles V, and Philip II. He is chiefly remembered for what is undoubtedly his finest achievement, the Palace of the Escorial, which makes great use of his trademark geometric decorative motifs.

Impressionism Extremely influential art movement that originated in France in the latter half of the 19th century and was to change the course of art forever. Its ethos was intensely personal, focusing on the artist and his response to the world around him, rather than on formal, academic representation of historical scenes. Favoured subjects were landscapes and vignettes of everyday life rather than grand tableaux, and colours were typically lighter than was traditional, and brushwork looser.

Jordaens , Jacob (1593–1678) Flemish painter whose style owes much to Rubens, with whom he collaborated frequently. A number of his works are in the Prado.

Maella, Mariano (1739–1819) Painter of the transition from the Baroque to the Neoclassical. Maella trained under Mengs, and became painter to the royal household, a post he shared with Goya. His output consists chiefly of portraits and religious works.

Meléndez, Luis (1716–80) Madrid-based painter of still lifes, perhaps the finest Spanish exponent of the genre. He was ill-rewarded for his talent, living and dying in penury.

Mengs, Anton Raphael (1728–79) Much acclaimed in his own lifetime, Mengs is a painter of the transition from the Baroque to the Neoclassical. Though his main work was done in Rome, he served two spells as painter to the court of Spain, and gained the ascendency over Tiepolo, whose adherence to the Baroque was seen as backward-looking.

Miró, Joan (1893–1983) Miró played around with the styles of the early 20th century, such as Fauvism and Cubism, meeting most of the major players, many of whom, like Miró himself, had gravitated to Paris. Himself a Catalan, Miró also drew on influences from Catalan folk art. In 1924 he entered the newly founded Surrealist School, though never quite fitted in with his peers; by the early 30s he had branched out on his own, conjuring up his own inimitable, instantly recognisable works, seemingly simplistic, with their vibrant colours and intense use of black. Many of these images are exhibited at the Reina Sofía.

Modernismo The Spanish name for Art Nouveau.

Mozarabic Term which describes the architecture of Christian Spain when the country was still under Moorish rule (9th–11th centuries).

Mudéjar A style of architecture which fuses elements of the Moorish and Gothic, found across Spain between the 12th and 16th centuries. The key manifestations include brickwork, marquetry and ceramics. Neo-Mudéjar was popular in the late 19th century.

Murillo, Bartolomé Esteban (1618–82) Born and almost entirely active in Seville, Murillo is nevertheless well represented in the Prado and in other museums in Madrid. His subject matter is mainly religious, painted in his trademark 'estilo vaporoso', a sort of soft-focus style which has led later critics to accuse him of dewy-eyed sentiment.

Neoclassicism Style of art and architecture that arose in response to the rediscovery of the art and architecture of the ancient world (Greece and Rome) and also as a reaction against the stagey excess of the Baroque and the flouncy frivolity of its successor, Rococo. Neoclassicism aspired to a serene purity of form and line, and a rational rather than emotional approach to subject matter.

Neo-Plasticism Term first used by Mondrian to describe severe, geometrical abstraction, in which no reference to the natural world is permitted.

Novecentismo The art of the 'nine hundreds', ie the 20th century, which flourished at the beginning of that century. Novecentismo was a reaction away from Modernismo (Art Nouveau) in favour of a more ordered, rational and Classical style.

Orphism An offshoot of Cubism aimed to be less harsh, with a less restricted colour palette and a more lyrical feel.

Oteiza, Jorge (1908–2003) Basque sculptor famous for his exploration of the void, of the role of the empty space in art. His *Empty Boxes* was one of his landmark works.

Pérez, Javier (b.1968) Exciting Basque artist, trained in Barcelona and Paris, who in a recent installation at the Palacio de Cristal created something ever so slightly reminiscent of certain Dalí paintings. Pérez, a keen depicter of the forms of the human body and the vagaries of the human mind, uses a wide range of unconventional materials, and also specialises in sculptures, drawings and videos.

Picasso, Pablo (1881–1973) The most famous of all modern artists needs little introduction. The full range of his pioneering styles, from his Blue and Pink Periods to Cubist and Abstract, are on show in Madrid. The Reina Sofía is not to be missed by Picasso fans: not just because it is home to what is perhaps his most famous work, *Guernica*, but also because its collection contains examples from the full range of his styles.

Plateresque Highly decorated style of architecture, with not an inch of space left uncarved, often seen on the façades of churches and public buildings, as a riot of ornament placed onto an unadorned space. It is unique to 16th-century Spain.

Pop Art Art movement born in the 1950s which took popular, consumer culture as its inspiration, using the icons of that culture (brand names, film stars, TV, motorcars) to create works that project that culture back at the viewer. The best known of all Pop Artists are Andy Warhol, Roy Lichtenstein, and—for sculpture—Claes Oldenberg.

Pórtico Art collective formed in 1947, and the first Spanish art movement to explore the Abstract as a medium for artistic expression. The group dissolved in 1952.

Raphael (Rafaello Sanzio; 1483–1520) Legendary painter of Madonnas and noted for his intricate but flamboyant work in the Vatican, Raphael was the youngest of the great trio of Italian High Renaissance artists, the others being Leonardo and Michelangelo. His early death at the age of 37 plunged the art world into deep mourning.

Ribera, José de (1591–1652) Almost all of Ribera's active life was spent in Italy, at a time when Naples was a Bourbon Spanish holding. He was a Caravaggist in style and temperament, known for his marked use of chiaroscuro and his ability to humanise religious and mythological subjects.

Ribera, Pedro de (1683—1742) Architect and notable exponent of the Churrigueresque. Named after its most famous practitioner, José Benito Churriguera, the term describes a riotously exuberant form of architecture which fuses elements of the Baroque with the plateresque. Ribera's most famous work in Madrid is the portal of the former Hospice of San Fernando (now the Museo Municipal), pictured on the back cover of this guide.

Rodríguez, Ventura (1717–85) Architect who took Spain into the Neoclassical era. Madrid's Palacio Real is his finest achievement.

Rubens, Peter Paul (1577–1640) Flemish titan of the very highest order, accredited with moving European art forward with his merging of the elaborate creativity of the Italian Renaissance with the Flemish Realism he grew up with. On visiting Spain, Rubens became friendly with Velázquez, and through that friendship is said to have influenced Spanish art development.

Sabatini, Francesco (1722–97) Italian architect who worked predominantly in Madrid. He was trained by his father-in-law, Luigi Vanvitelli, with whom he collaborated with in the construction of the Palacio de Caserta in Naples. It was in Naples (then a Bourbon holding) that he was headhunted by the future Carlos III and was one of that king's architectural heralds of the new Madrid, employed by the king in his bid to put the relatively backward-looking Spanish capital on a visual par with other European cities. Neoclassical in style, Sabatini's work draws more on the Italian Renaissance than on the ancient world. In 1769 he saw off competition from Ventura Rodríguez and José de Hermosilla to design Puerta de Alcalá, one of Madrid's best known landmarks.

Saura, Antonio (b. 1930) Expressionist artist of an intensely powerful, often disturbing vision, using sometimes religious imagery to depict the sufferings of captive humanity. He was an outspoken opponent of the Franco régime.

Sorolla, Joaquín (1863–1923) Valencia-born artist known for his attractive genre scenes and social pieces, and more especially for his particular use of light. Known as *luminismo*, his technique infuses his works with vivid Mediterranean sunshine. The Museo Sorolla in Madrid, his former home, possesses a fine collection of his paintings.

Surrealism Art movement established by André Breton in 1924 out of the remnants of Dada, drawing also on aspects of Cubism. The movement explored the unconscious mind, delivering elusive and ground-breaking works conjured up by both sheer fantasy and dream-like visions. There are many works on show in Madrid from the movement's key proponents, especially Max Ernst, Joan Miró, René Magritte, and—last but certainly not least—Salvador Dalí, the most famous Surrealist, though out on a limb a little, as his right-wing political stance distanced him from his leftist peers. Surrealism was also influenced by the dream-like fantasies that have pervaded art from Bosch and Arcimboldo to Goya. Works by all these artists can also be found in Madrid.

Tàpies, Antoni (b.1923) This abstract pioneer is widely regarded as Spain's greatest living artist and was one of the founders of Dau el Set in 1948. He achieved worldwide fame for his highly original works derived from the inventive mixing of paint, cloth and metal, which had an explicit influence on the Arte Povera movement. He set up the important art museum and art resource centre Fundació Tàpies in his native Barcelona in 1987.

Tiepolo, Giovanni Battista (1696–1770) Venetian genius of the Baroque who spent his last years in Madrid as court painter to Carlos III. His *Apotheosis of Spain* adorns the Throne Room in the Palacio Real. His final years were poisoned by jealousy of Mengs, whose new Neoclassical style meant that he eclipsed the older master in fame and reputation.

Titian (Tiziano Vecellio; c. 1485–1576) The greatest artist of the Venetian School, and a towering figure of the Renaissance, known for his use of colour, which is sumptuous and thoughtful by turns. He was an important influence on Velázquez. His portrait of Philip II of Spain, painted before the young prince ascended the throne, launched a lifelong passion for his work on the part of the monarch. Philip's superb collection of Titians is an important part of the Prado holding.

Vallecas School Important avant-garde art movement founded in Spain before the Civil War, and unique in that it managed to continue into the Franco era. Its most famous members were Benjamín Palencia and Alberto Sánchez, whose works can be seen in the Reina Sofía. The Vallecas manifesto was to bring Spanish art into the modern age, and to put it on a par with that of France.

Velázquez, Diego (1599–1660) In 1623 Velázquez painted a portrait of Felipe IV that so delighted his royal sitter that he became the king's favoured artist. Instantly he left tawdry genre scenes behind him, concentrating on portaiture and history painting, creating masterpieces such as *Las Meninas* and *The Surrender of Breda* (both in the Prado) which secured his place as the greatest artist of the Spanish School. Manet regarded him as the greatest artist of all time.

Vicente, Esteban (1903–2001) Spanish-born Abstract Expressionist artist who studied with Dalí, and counted Picasso and Miró among his friends. He emigrated to the US in 1936.

Villanueva, Juan de (1739–1811) Architect noted for taking Spain out of the Baroque and into the Neoclassical era. His patrons were Carlos III and Carlos IV, under whom he produced the finest of all Spanish Neoclassical buildings, the Prado.

Zurbarán, Francisco de (1598–1664) Important contemporary of Velázquez, chiefly known for his powerful portraits of friars and saints, painted against a plain background, radiating emotion and humanity. He was highly successful as a young man, and much loved by the arbiters of the Counter Reformation, who approved of his plainness and piety. In middle age he was overtaken in popularity by fellow-Sevillan Murillo, and died in financial difficulty.

index

Numbers in italics are picture references. Numbers in bold refer to the art glossary.

Photo editor: Róbert Szabó Benke

Front cover: Ceramic tile representation of *Los Borrachos* by Velázquez, on the Los Gabrieles bar. Photo by Phil Robinson

Back cover: Façade of the Museo Municipal by Pedro de Ribera. Reproduced by courtesy of the Museo Municipal de Madrid; © de la fotografía Museo Municipal de Madrid

For permission to reproduce artwork throughout the book, grateful thanks are due to the following:

Bridgeman Art Library (pp. 28, 140, 161. Image on p. 28 ©HUNGART 2005); Carmen Thyssen-Bornemisza Collection (p. 42); Ermita de San Antonio de la Florida y Museo Panteón de Goya (p. 112); Fundación Lázaro Galdiano (p. 136); Museo Municipal de Madrid (pp. 105, 106, back cover); Museo Nacional del Prado (pp. 14, 20); Palacio Real de Madrid (p. 73)

Other photographs by:

Hadley Kincade (pp. 56, 70, 83, 85, 87, 91, 96, 121, 123, 154, 164);

Phil Robinson (pp. 46, 53, 79, 81, 92, 99, 125, 168, 170, front cover & gatefold)

art/shop/eat Madrid
First edition 2005

Published by Somerset Kft, a Somerset Books company
Lövőház utca 39, 1024 Budapest, Hungary
www.blueguides.com

ISBN 963-867-27-06

Published in the United States of America by
W.W. Norton & Company Inc
500 Fifth Avenue, New York, NY 10110, USA

ISBN 0-393-32834-1

A Blue Guides publication
Series devised by Gemma Davies

Layout and production: Anikó Kuzmich
Repro Studio: Timp Kft.
Floorplans by Imre Bába, ©Somerset Kft
Maps by Dimap Bt.
Felelős kiadó: Ruszin Zsolt, a Somerset Kft. igazgatója

Printed and bound in China by M.G.I. Print

SOMERSET BOOKS

art/shop/eat
BARCELONA

art/shop/eat
FLORENCE

art/shop/eat
LONDON

art/shop/eat
NEW YORK

art/shop/eat
PARIS

art/shop/eat
ROME

art / shop / eat